"In an increasingly interactive world knowledge of how networks operate and evolve, and how they can be managed effectively, is increasingly important to students and practitioners of public administration, public management and public policy. In the first edition of this excellent book, the authors developed the idea of "process management" – contrasting it with other forms of such as "project-based" management – highlighting the advantages of using a process lens as a guide to producing better public sector outcomes. In this thoroughly revised and expanded new edition, the authors continue this pursuit, adding detail and nuance to their analyses of the best (and not-so-good) strategies that can be used to enhance collaboration between public, civil society and other actors in the pursuit of public value and the public good."
Michael Howlett, *Burnaby Mountain Chair, Department of Political Science, Simon Fraser University and Professor, Lee Kuan Yew School of Public Policy, National University of Singapore*

"*Management in Networks* (second edition) is a fundamental guide for policy makers and managers who wants to consciously decide and act in today's uncertain and complex world, where all decisions involve many actors, with different values and targets."
Giovanni Azzone, *Professor of Management and Rector Emeritus, Politecnico di Milano, Italy*

"Theories of management and decision-making abound, but how do we put these into practice? The new edition of this classic book reveals all the nuts and bolts to both practitioners and scientists."
Lasse Gerrits, *Professor for the Governance of Complex and Innovative Technological Systems, Otto-Friedrich University Bamberg, Germany*

"Hans de Bruijn and Ernst ten Heuvelhof show how management can deal with uncertainty. Their incredibly valuable 'rules of the game' for networked decision-making allow for the outcome of the process to emerge and for actors to subsequently ascribe coherence."
Arthur Petersen, *Professor of Science, Technology and Public Policy, University College London*

Management in Networks

Getting what you want – even if you are the boss – isn't always easy. Almost every organisation, big or small, works among a network of competing interests. Whether these are governments pushing through policies, companies trying to increase profits, or even families deciding where to move house, rarely can decisions be made in isolation from competing interests both within the organisation and outside it.

In this accessible and straightforward account, Hans de Bruijn and Ernst ten Heuvelhof cast light on multi-stakeholder decision-making. Using plain language, they reveal the nuts and bolts of decision-making within the numerous dilemmas and tensions at work. Drawing on a diverse range of illustrative examples throughout, their perceptive analysis examines how different interests can either support or block change, and the strategies available for managing a variety of stakeholders.

The second edition of *Management in Networks* incorporates a wider spread of international cases, a new chapter giving an overview of different network types, and a new chapter looking at digital governance and the impact of big data on networks.

This insightful text is invaluable reading for students of management and organisational studies, plus practitioners – or actors – operating in a range of contexts.

Hans de Bruijn is Professor of Organisation and Management at Delft University of Technology, the Netherlands. His research is on networked, multi-actor governance, both between and within organisations.

Ernst ten Heuvelhof is Professor of Public Administration at Delft University of Technology, the Netherlands. His research focuses on decision-making by actors – both public and private – who operate in networks and have diverse interests.

Management in Networks

Second edition

Hans de Bruijn and Ernst ten Heuvelhof

Routledge
Taylor & Francis Group

LONDON AND NEW YORK

Second edition published 2018
by Routledge
2 Park Square, Milton Park, Abingdon, Oxon OX14 4RN

and by Routledge
711 Third Avenue, New York, NY 10017

Routledge is an imprint of the Taylor & Francis Group, an informa business

First edition published by Routledge 2008

British Library Cataloguing in Publication Data
A catalogue record for this book is available from the British Library

Library of Congress Cataloging in Publication Data
Names: Bruijn, J. A. de, 1962- author. | Heuvelhof, E. F. ten (Ernst F.),
    author.
Title: Management in networks / Hans de Bruijn and Ernst ten Heuvelhof.
Description: Second Edition. | New York : Routledge, 2018. | Revised
    edition of the authors' Management in networks, 2008.
Identifiers: LCCN 2017045943| ISBN 9781138211421 (hbk) | ISBN
    9781138211438 (pbk) | ISBN 9781315453019 (ebk)
Subjects: LCSH: Decision making. | Organizational behavior. |
    Organizational sociology.
Classification: LCC HD30.23 .B777 2008 | DDC 658.4/036–dc23
LC record available at https://lccn.loc.gov/2017045943

ISBN: 978-1-138-21142-1 (hbk)
ISBN: 978-1-138-21143-8 (pbk)
ISBN: 978-1-315-45301-9 (ebk)

Typeset in Times New Roman
by Taylor & Francis Books

Printed and bound by CPI Group (UK) Ltd, Croydon, CR0 4YY

Contents

List of illustrations

Figures

Tables

Preface

This book is about decision-making and change processes in our interconnected world.

In an interconnected world with many players, often with wicked problems and with plenty of dynamism, decision-making or change is often nonlinear and erratic. Sometimes decision-making even seems like a chaotic process, where no single pattern can be recognised.

In this book we unravel decision-making and show that there are patterns in this seemingly messy process. We describe the strategies of the players involved in decision-making. We show to what results the sum of these strategies lead – how they impact processes of decision-making and change. We not only describe and analyse these strategies and processes, but we also answer the question concerning what effective strategies there are for making decisions and creating change in an interconnected world. Many of these insights are contraintuitive for those who believe in linear, project-based decision-making.

This book is intended for anyone interested in decision-making and change, particularly for those who are subject experts in a specific area – whether that is infrastructure or the environment, safety or innovation – and who are surprised every time by the chaotic process of decision-making.

Hans de Bruijn
Ernst ten Heuvelhof

1 Our interconnected world and what it means for decision and policy making

An interconnected world

We live in an interconnected world (Castells, 2011). The internet and the globalisation of the economy mean everything is connected to everything else. That sometimes has unforeseen and dramatic consequences. Take, for example, the economic crisis at the beginning of the twenty-first century. The fact that Europe is a system of interconnected economies is why problems in the small Greek economy could throw the entire euro zone into crisis. The housing bubble in America caused a global economic crisis. Cybercrime is an international game played out in a web of technology and actors in which the villains are thousands of kilometres away from their victims.

Chaos theory uses a well-known metaphor to clarify these processes in an interconnected world: the 'butterfly effect'. A butterfly in Brazil flaps its wings and causes a tornado in Texas months later. The initial movement – the flap of the butterfly's wings – causes only a tiny effect. But that is just the first of a chain of effects that gets bigger and bigger until eventually a tornado develops in Texas. Who imagines in advance that a butterfly, thousands of kilometres away, could cause a tornado? Who had ever thought that the small Greek economy could send the entire euro zone into a crisis? These are phenomena that are inherent to an interconnected world and that in many cases we can only recognise in hindsight rather than predict in advance.

In this book we will discuss the question of what this interconnected world means for change processes, for policy-making and for decision-making. In a nutshell: What does it mean for governance? It will become clear that a linear, systematic approach to governance is impossible in an interconnected world. So, the question is, how can governance be made possible?

Toward this end, in this first chapter we will unravel the essence of an interconnected world. How is this world structured, and what does this structure mean for the progress of decision-making processes in networks? With the help of these insights we can then, in the following chapters of this book, explore how governance can be substantiated in an interconnected world.

The structure of an interconnected world: three characteristics

Table 1.1 shows the three most important characteristics of the interconnected world – at least if we look at them from the perspective of governance.

First characteristic: Interdependencies

The first important characteristic of an interconnected world is that, indeed, it is inhabited by a large number of parties or actors (we will use both these terms alternately throughout this book): governments, companies, not-for-profit organisations, citizens. These actors have differing interests and are dependent on each other. These interdependencies are inherent to a high-tech society with its super-specialisms: the more specialisms, the more dependencies, – including its dependence on the internet. In the web of dependencies thus created nobody can achieve anything without the support of others. These interdependencies result in a multitude of relationships between the actors. Together all these relationships form what we call a network.

The world as a whole has become a network, but nations, regions and local communities are equally a network. When decisions must be taken, for example about roads or airports, we very often see that many local players, with differing interests, are involved. In this context, think of certain organisations, such as municipalities, companies, local action groups and environmentalists. However, the impact of the network concept goes even further. Even the organisations that form the actors in a network are often networks themselves. An organisation such as a hospital, a law firm or an engineering consultancy comprises highly trained professionals, with very different specialisms, who are dependent on each other. The professionals are dependent on the management, but the management is equally dependent on the professionals who possess the expertise and knowledge the managers do not have.

A network can be ideal-typed as the opposite of a hierarchy. A hierarchy is a vertical, pyramid-like structure in which there is a person or group that is in charge and that ultimately makes the decisions. All the other actors are subordinate to this group or person, so there are vertical relationships of superordination and subordination. In a network there is no such thing as a vertical structure. There are many players, nobody can say that he or she is 'in charge', and the relationships are horizontal not vertical.

Table 1.1 Main characteristics of an interconnected world

Characteristic of an interconnected world	*… instead of*
Interdependencies	Hierarchy
Unstructured 'wicked' problems	Structured problems
Dynamics	Stability

To understand the complexity of the network of interdependencies a number of other characteristics of networks are important.

Types of interdependencies

In the first place: interdependencies can take all kinds of forms.

- Bilateral or multilateral dependencies: Dependencies can exist between two parties but also between more than two parties.
- Single or multidimensional dependencies: Dependencies can relate to one dimension (for example, money) but also to several dimensions (money, information, authorities, relationships).
- Synchronous versus asynchronous dependencies: Actors can at one point in time all be mutually dependent on each other, but the dependencies can also be spread out over time. Today the first actor is dependent on the second actor, but a few months later this second actor is dependent on the first actor.
- Static versus dynamic dependencies. A dependency is dynamic if it changes over the course of time. A party can occupy a dominant position in a network, but that dominant position can become stronger or weaker as time goes by. A static dependency is not subject to change.

In many networks of interdependencies the dependencies are multilateral, multidimensional, asynchronous and dynamic. That makes decision-making and changes in these networks extremely complex, but we'll come back to that later.

Different interdependencies per topic

A second important aspect of interdependencies is that they can differ per topic. We can use a regional authority as an example. The regional authority is dependent on municipalities, the central government and private parties – and all these actors are, in turn, dependent on the regional authority. The 'region' focuses on physical infrastructure, which involves many different parties who together form a network of interdependencies. In this network the region has a degree of dominance, but the region also deals with nature and the environment. Once again other parties are also involved – some are the same as for infrastructure, some are different – and in this network the region may not have the same degree of dominance. As a result the decision-making processes in the infrastructure network and the nature and environment network may be very different. It may also be the case that certain parties are involved in both networks and this can also influence the decision-making. Coming off the worst in the decision-making regarding infrastructure can affect a party's attitude when it comes to decisions about nature and the environment. This makes decision-making more complex, not only because the network differs per issue but also because certain parties will want to link the decision-making related to one issue to the decision-making related to the other issue.

Interdependencies don't always reveal themselves

The interdependencies have already created a very complex picture: There are many kinds of dependencies, they can differ per topic, and some people link these topics together. We can add a third factor into the mix: Not all the actors in a network always know what the reciprocal dependencies are. For example, a region may think a municipality holds a weak position in a network whereas, in fact, it holds a very strong position. A region may not know, or may not know with sufficient precision, an actor's views of and interests in a network. Certainly when it comes to more complex networks (many actors, many kinds of dependencies and many links to other networks), it is virtually impossible for a single actor to oversee the entire network. If actors are unsure of the position of other actors in a network – position not only in terms of dominance but also in terms of views and interests – it goes without saying that an actor's perception of the positions of others may be mistaken. A party could be more dominant than expected and a wrong assessment of a party's power can make the decision-making far more complicated. Different actors can, therefore, also have different perceptions regarding the positions in a network. That, too, does not render decision-making simpler.

Networks of interdependencies are already complex, but they become even more complex when the actors involved can have very different perceptions of the same network.

Second characteristic: Unstructured, wicked problems

A second characteristic of an interconnected world concerns the content of the problems that must be solved in such a world. These problems are often 'unstructured' or 'wicked' (Rittel & Webber, 1973). Unstructured problems can be ideal-typed as the opposite of structured problems, which are problems for which there is only one right, or the right, solution. An example of a structured problem is the question, "What does 1+1 make?" The answer is 2 – and that answer is independent of political preferences, interests or dominance. Unstructured problems do not have a single right answer. Why are so many problems unstructured?

To explain this we will use a simple example. A dairy company wants to know which type of packaging for milk is the most environmentally responsible: a cardboard carton, a glass bottle with a deposit or a polycarbonate bottle with a deposit. The dairy company wants to know how each of the three types of packaging scores for what are called the 'environmental components': energy usage, water usage, toxicity and waste.

To answer this question, several factors must be inventoried, including the production process of these three types of packaging: Which raw materials are used, and how they are transformed into a packaging? Take the cardboard carton. This requires that a tree be cut down somewhere and then transported to a factory where it is turned into cardboard. The cardboard then goes to a factory where it is made into a carton, and other materials, such as a plastic (polyethylene) coating, are added. The polyethylene has also undergone its own production process, which began with cracking naphtha, so that must also be inventoried.

Let's suppose the tree is cut down in Sweden, transported to Hamburg to be made into cardboard and then the cardboard goes to a factory in Switzerland where it is made into cartons, and other components, such as the polyethylene coating, are added. To determine the real environmental impact, we must make at least three decisions.

- What data are we going to use? We need, for example, data regarding the number of trees that must be cut down to produce a specified number of cartons. We need data regarding the transportation of the trees: How much energy did it cost?
- Which system boundaries will we apply? Or, to put it another way: How do we demarcate the investigation? The trees are transported by ship. We want to know how much energy that costs. But because maybe there wouldn't be a ship without trees,, must we now also include the building of the ship when determining the environmental cost of the packaging?
- How do we allocate environmental impact to the packaging? The ship also transports cars and washing machines, so what portion of the necessary energy should be allocated to the washing machines and cars and what portion to the trees?

There are many other questions that could be asked, but in this context what it comes down to is that there isn't an objective answer to many of the questions. One party opts for one data set, the other party prefers other data set. One party opts for system boundaries that the other party considers too narrow or too wide. The allocation could also be calculated using various different methods.

Let's now suppose that, when deciding on the packaging, our dairy company has to deal with all kinds of other parties, such as an environmental organisation, a governmental authority and several consumer organisations, and that all these parties have different interests and different opinions about the three decisions to be made. The result can be a major conflict regarding the question of the right data, system boundaries and allocation methods – making an objective answer often impossible. When that is the case, many parties will have a tendency to make choices that suit their own interests or preferences.

But, let's suppose these parties agree about the data, system boundaries and methods, so they know how the three packaging options score for the environmental components energy usage, water usage, toxicity and waste.

Then we come to the next question: how to weigh the four factors against each other. Is a packaging with a bad score for water and waste, but a good score for energy, better than a packaging that scores bad for energy but excellent for water and neutral for waste? To a great extent this is a normative question – and about this question, too, different parties can have very different opinions without there being any objective judgement in respect of the 'right' answer. Think about it: So far we have only looked at the environmental aspects. There are many other aspects, such as safety and cost. How do you deal with a packaging that scores well for environmental impact and cost, but badly for safety issues? That makes it all even more complicated.

The essence of all this is:

- The facts we need to enable us to reach a good decision can either be clear-cut or ambiguous.
- The normative considerations we must weigh in order to reach a good decision may be either objective or subjective.

When the facts are ambiguous and the normative consideration is difficult or impossible to objectify, the result is an unstructured problem. See Table 1.2.

When unstructured problems have to be solved in a network with many actors all with different interests, there is a good chance the actors will disagree about data, system boundaries, methods and the normative weight of different components. Their interests often play a role in this – the manufacturer of one-time-use cardboard packaging looks at environmental analyses in a different way than the manufacturer of reusable polycarbonate bottles. In view of their interest the two manufacturers will be critical of analyses with, for them, disagreeable outcomes. This is not, therefore, merely an outright defence of their own interest – when it comes to unstructured problems, the facts don't speak for themselves, so there is scope for them to be discussed.

Third characteristic: Dynamics

A third characteristic of the interconnected world is that it is dynamic – the interconnected world is constantly in motion. Dynamic can be ideal-typed as the opposite of stable.

Here, too, we will start with an example. The decision-making related to large infrastructure projects often involves many parties, including some who

Table 1.2 Unstructured problems

	Facts: objectifiable	*Facts: not objectifiable*
Normative consideration: objectifiable		
Normative consideration: not objectifiable		Unstructured problem

support such a project and some who are against it. This can be the case if, for example, a harbour authority wants to build an offshore port. What is the dynamic that can emerge in this network of interdependencies?

In the first place this dynamic can be due to the behaviour of the actors in the network. The decision-making starts with a number of actors, but new actors can join the decision-making later. Maybe there is a seaside resort, and the resort's mayor realises the offshore port could have a negative effect on local tourism. The resort can involve itself in the decision-making and demand compensation or a new design for the offshore port. Some actors will leave the network because, on reflection, they have less interest in the decision-making.

In the second place it could be the content of the problem – in this case the construction of an offshore port – that is dynamic. The problem content can shift. In many cases, projects like these are initially classified as economic infrastructure projects, but it's possible that during the decision-making process it becomes apparent that the port could also play a role in protecting the coast from a rising sea level. Configured in a particular way the offshore port could result in natural land reclamation and thus contribute towards coastal protection.

This shifts the problem's content from a purely economic infrastructure issue to an issue that also includes coastal protection and ecology. Naturally this shift means other actors, with other interests, appear on the scene and the decision-making process changes.

These two types of dynamics – actors and content – can reinforce each other. When actors, each with their own definition of the problem, enter or exit the scene, the problem's content will constantly shift. When the problem content shifts, new actors come on the scene, and the positions in the network change. When the two developments – changing actors and changing content – reinforce each other, a dynamic situation can degenerate into a chaotic situation. But, behind this chaos there is a pattern – dynamics related to actors and dynamics related to content.

Decision-making in an interconnected world

Decision-making processes are played out within the network structure we have sketched. Before we explain these processes, let's introduce an illustration that can help us understand these differences: the dancing table.

The dancing table

In a large house there is a large room with four corners – A, B, C and D – with a table in the middle. There are two people in the room – P1 and P2.

Both P1 and P2 have an opinion regarding the corner in which the table should stand. P1 wants it in corner A, P2 in corner B.

P1 and P2 set to work: They push and pull the table towards the corner in which they each want it to stand. P1 pushes it towards A, and P2 pushes it towards B.

What happens to the table? If P1 and P2 are equally strong and they both push and pull at the same time, the table will move but not towards either A or B. The table will eventually come to rest against one of the room's walls, halfway between A and B at point E.

Are P1 and P2 happy with this result? P1 may say that the table is now nearer to A, but he has to admit he failed to get the table into corner A. And maybe he will add a comment: If I, P1, haven't got what I want, maybe the other person, P2, has got what he wants. But it's very possible that P2 also feels that he hasn't gotten what he wants while P1 has.

This illustrates the dissatisfaction that is so characteristic of complex decision-making processes. This dissatisfaction has an absolute and a relative dimension. In absolute terms P1 and P2 are dissatisfied. Indeed, they both realise they haven't achieved their goal and are not happy. On top of that, in relative terms, they are dissatisfied in respect to their opponent. Both P1 and P2 could argue that the other has gained the most. It doesn't need to be explained that this conclusion makes a person unhappy: They've worked hard but not achieved their goals while the opponent has achieved more.

What's going on? The table has ended up at E. This outcome is due to the efforts of P1 and P2, but it's not the outcome for which either of them was aiming. Neither P1 nor P2 had E in mind as the desired outcome. Outcome E is the result of two forces – a force pushing towards A and a force pushing towards B. Although the process involved a lot of effort, what happened in the end was not what anyone thought, wanted or planned. The result is *emergent* – it has arisen unplanned. In a situation in which two different parties push a table in different directions neither will get what they want, and a party may mistakenly believe that not getting what they want means the other party has gotten what it wants.

Up to this point it's been a very simple process: The assumptions were that only two people were involved, and both of them started and finished their activities at the same time. Let's make this assumption more realistic.

Let's suppose there are ten parties – P1 to P10 – all of whom want the table in one of the corners of the room.

We'll also make the second assumption more realistic. The parties don't all start and stop pushing and pulling at the same time, instead they get involved in the process at different times. If the table moves in a particular direction as a result of the pushing and pulling of the participating actors, there will be other actors who consider this movement a reason to become involved. It may be because they are unhappy about the direction in which the table is moving, or it may be because, having seen which way the table is moving, they see an opportunity for themselves opening up and, therefore, wade in and join the scrum of pushing and pulling actors. There will also be actors who call it quits at some point. This may be because they are happy with the result achieved thus far, or it may be because, having seen the position of the table and the direction in which it is moving, they realise their mission is unachievable. It's also conceivable that their priorities suddenly change, and their new priorities mean they must leave this room to go into action in a different room. But other actors return – the table has once again become a priority for them. The result of all this will be dynamics: The actors come and go, each of them at, for him, an opportune moment.

What happens to the table if many actors are pushing and pulling it, with everyone starting and stopping at different times? The table will move hither and thither around the room. Now to the left, then back towards the right, depending on who is pushing and pulling at that moment. Sometimes the table will be static for a moment – the forces are precisely balanced against each other. At other times the table will move quickly in a straight line – the participating parties are in agreement and are single-mindedly pushing in the same direction – but looked at over a longer period the table's course through the room will be erratic. It will dance around the room from one side to the other. The pushing and pulling of every party will have some influence on the course the table follows, but no single party has a determining influence on what happens to the table.

So there you have the example of the dancing table. The example helps to illustrate the characteristics of decision-making in networks. How do these decision-making characteristics compare with those in a hierarchy? As was mentioned earlier, in a hierarchy there is one actor who is in charge, problems are often structured, and there is a certain degree of stability. By contrast, in a network there are many actors, none of whom are in charge, problems are unstructured, and there are dynamics.

Unstructured, nonlinear decision-making instead of structured, linear decision-making

When there is one actor who is in charge, the decision-making process can be structured and linear. Decision-making starts with the formulation of a problem and the determining of goals (in fact, the problem and goals of the hierarchically highest placed actor). The problem is then divided into sub-problems, information is gathered, and a decision is made. The decision is then implemented and evaluated.

When decision-making has to take place in a network, this always means that different actors are involved in the process. These actors have different interests and are dependent on each other. This means no actor is in a position to solve the problem alone. The actors must work together in order to achieve their own goals. A decision-making process is only effective if it is carried out jointly – which doesn't go without saying because actors have differing interests.

The major consequence of all this is that decision-making processes are often erratic and unstructured – just like the dancing table. Table 1.3 shows the most important differences

Table 1.3 Comparison of decision-making in a hierarchy and in a network

Hierarchy	Network
Structured and linear	Unstructured and nonlinear
Phased	Random
Actors' behaviour is strategy-led	Actors' behaviour is content-led
A single arena: The process has clear starting and finishing points	Multiple arenas: no single starting or finishing point
Problem content stable	Problem content shifts
Incentive to view the problem as structured	Incentive to view the problem as unstructured
Constancy and predictability	Inconstancy and unpredictability

Decision-making in irregular rounds instead of regular phases

The picture of a decision-making process that proceeds in a regular and linear manner can, partly due to this, be replaced by the picture of a process that proceeds in *rounds* (Teisman, 2000). Think of a boxing match. During a round of fighting the actors reach a decision or maybe do their utmost to prevent a decision from being reached. A round ends at some point and delivers an interim result, including winners and losers. It looks as if the decision-making is over, but a new round can be announced without any warning. An actor who thought he or she had won, or was at least in a winning position, may see their win being washed away in the second round. Think of the dancing table. At a particular moment it may be in corner C. For many of the parties, this is an undesirable outcome. Why shouldn't they wait a while and then try to move the table out of this corner again? The process may appear to be concluded, but suddenly a new round can begin, with a new balance of power.

Strategic behaviour, not just content, determines the behaviour

Actors can act strategically – they can play a clever game. An experienced actor, who knows that decision-making progresses in rounds, can adapt his behaviour to suit this knowledge. He can, for example, decide to hold back during the first rounds and accept a loss because he knows, from experience, that the game is decided during the later rounds. Or it could be that an actor knows the table will end up in a corner. The first time this happens, some of the parties will be so disappointed that they immediately announce a second round. If this is a kind of natural law – the first time the table goes into a corner it doesn't stay there for long – a party can anticipate this by saving his strength for the second round. If many of the parties behave this way, it makes the decision-making more dynamic. Another known scenario is that actors only become *active* during the *tail-end* of a decision-making process: They see which solution is likely to be selected, have problems with this and endeavour to block or redirect further decision-making.

Multiple arenas not one arena, and processes don't have clear starting and finishing points

Let's go back to the room with the dancing table. Perhaps one of the parties in the room with the dancing table is willing to help an opponent in return for the opponent helping her with a totally different problem that is being played out in another room. The parties who help their opponents are, as far as the final position of the table is concerned, losers: The table won't end up where they want it to end up. But, these losers will be compensated by the winners when it comes to a different problem in a subsequent decision-making process and in a different room.

The example teaches us two things. In a network decision-making often takes place in multiple arenas. The parties in the room with the table meet each other in other rooms for other decision-making processes. The different decision-making processes are interwoven. The outcome in the room with the dancing table cannot be understood without knowledge of the processes in the other rooms. As a result, no decision-making process has a clear-cut starting and finishing point. The table ends up in a particular corner, but the decision-making process in the next room carries on.

The problem content shifts rather than being stable

When we then look at how the content of the decision-process develops in networks, what stands out is that the content constantly changes. The *content* of a *problem* appears *to shift* as time goes by (Kingdon, 1984).

Actors redefine their problems as time goes by. They do this because at a particular moment the problems as they had originally formulated them are not receiving sufficient support from the network. The classical view is that a problem arises and requires a solution, but the problem of the dancing table is apparently unsolvable. Perhaps other problems that *are* solvable are being played out in other rooms. In one other room a cupboard has to be moved. In yet another room a wall has to be painted. Actors in a network will, at some point, make a strategic assessment regarding which problems have a chance of being solved and which don't. There is no solution for the problem of the table; there might well be a solution for the problem of the wall that needs painting. In that case the sensible thing to do would be to concentrate on the problem in the room to be painted and, for the time being at least, to move the problem of the table in the corner to the bottom of the agenda.

Incentives to define a problem as unstructured

As we've said, problems are unstructured, or wicked, if:

- The facts needed to enable a good decision to be reached are ambiguous rather than clear-cut; and

- The normative considerations that must be weighed in order to reach a good decision cannot be objective.

In a network with many different actors there are significant incentives to define a problem as unstructured. The minute a problem is unstructured, the actors in the network have room to manoeuvre. They need not be as bound by the information because the information is ambiguous. The normative considerations are open to discussion in order to reach a good decision.

How can a structured problem be turned into an unstructured problem? Take the example of someone driving through a red light and this being recorded on a traffic camera.

The facts are clear. There is also a consensus regarding the accepted norms: Legislation and regulations stipulate that driving through a red light is an offence and specify the penalty. The problem is, therefore, structured and easy to solve: The driver is fined. The relationship between the authorities and this driver is hierarchic.

Now suppose that the driver engages a lawyer. This activates the conflict of interests between the authorities and the driver. What will the lawyer's strategy be? He will endeavour to change the consensus regarding the facts: Yes, the traffic light was red, but there was a seriously ill person lying on the back seat of the car. And, on top of that, it was the middle of the night, and there was hardly any traffic on the road. He will also try to affect the consensus regarding the accepted norms. In this case two norms are involved: the norm that driving through a red light is an offence and the norm that necessity knows no law. If the lawyer's endeavours succeed, the problem has suddenly become unstructured, and there is room for negotiation, for example regarding the severity of the fine.

The thrust of this story: A problem is made unstructured by broadening its scope because that means additional information is required. And additional information leads to more ambiguity. It also means more values come into the picture, and that leads to even less structure. The more unstructured a problem, the more room to manoeuvre for the parties in the network.

Unpredictability and no consistency

The previously mentioned dynamics related to the actors and the content of the decision-making means that new and unforeseen situations arise continuously. In a hierarchy consistency is an important value: Once goals and plans have been formulated, they should be achieved. Due to its dynamics, in a network consistency can obstruct the achievement of goals. An actor should, in fact, have the capacity to shift with the decision-making and identify and utilise opportunities. In a hierarchy decision-making is predictable: To a great extent the goals and preconditions determine the progress of the decision-making. In a network decision-making is, in principle, unpredictable. In a nutshell, the dynamics of networks invite actors to adapt their behaviour to these dynamics, which reinforces them.

Conclusion: decision-making proceeds erratically

The conclusion based on the above has to be that decision-making proceeds far more erratically in a network than it does in a hierarchical structure. This unpredictability is the most important regularity in decision-making processes and can be traced back to two components:

- Content unpredictability: A problem's content and solution shift continuously and, in addition, solutions can determine the problem's definition rather than the other way round. New problems and solutions can be brought in during the decision-making process, and existing problems and solutions can be eliminated.
- Process unpredictability: The decision-making has no clear starting and finishing points and proceeds in rounds, which follow each other irregularly. The process has no clearly distinct phases, such as is suggested in many consultancy-type and project-based models. There is also no logical sequence of problem signalling via analyses and decision-making regarding a solution to be implemented. In models the decision-making progresses in a linear fashion; in practice decision-making is a meandering process.

Decision-making in a network: barriers and opportunities

To summarise, in a world in which unstructured problems are dealt with in dynamic networks, decision-making will ostensibly be chaotic and shambolic. That sounds like a sombre message, but in the following chapters it will be made clear that there are strategies for ensuring that decision-making processes in these networks are effective. In this section the core question is not only what barriers to decision-making and changes in networks are there, but also what opportunities do networks offer for achieving decision-making and changes.

In networks there are many different parties with different interests. These parties are mutually dependent. What does this diversity and these interdependencies mean for actors who want to bring about a change? What barriers and opportunities do they provide?

Barriers

Suppose there is an actor who wants to change something and towards this end he initiates an intervention. With what barriers will this actor be confronted due to the variety or diversity in a network (Cameron, 1986; Morgan, 1986, p.190ff; Peters, 1998; Quinn & Rohrbaugh, 1983)?

Limited impact and success of the intervention

In the first place, the more variety within a network the less impact and success an actor's intervention will have. Variety naturally means that every party in a network is receptive to a different type of intervention. Suppose, for example, that a minister of the environment makes agreements with a particular business sector regarding environmental performance. Then suppose that this sector is very diverse: The companies differ in size and profitability; the technical possibilities for environmental improvement differ greatly from one company to the next; and some of the companies have a good *past performance* record in respect to environmental measures and have already achieved a great deal, while other companies have so far invested almost nothing in environmental improvements.

Due to this variety, the agreement can lead to different reactions from the different companies. It is, for example, conceivable that larger companies will find compliance easier than small companies; that companies with a low profitability or with few technological possibilities for environmental improvement will withdraw from the agreements; and that companies with a good environmental past performance will have more problems with making yet more improvements than companies that thus far have not implemented any environmental measures.

The diversity in the sector is, therefore, limiting the impact and success of the intervention. It's quite likely that there is good cohesion between the agreements and only a handful of the companies due to their characteristics. At all the other companies there are all kinds of poor fits, which could lead to the intervention having unforeseen effects.

Variety requires tail made interventions – but pushes the boundaries
of manageability

A logical reaction to diversity is to opt for differentiation and tailor-made interventions: The intervention is tuned to the specific characteristics of the involved parties.

A second obstacle for change is that such interventions can soon be pushing the boundaries of manageability.

We'll take a simple example. Suppose that the board of an organisation with a variety of business units wants to reduce absence due to sickness. Even such a simple goal can be difficult to achieve in this type of organisation. There can be major differences between the units that influence the absenteeism: the nature of the work, the average age of the employees, the number of cases of long-term illness (which can raise the average), the registration method, etc. Here a tailor-made intervention means that separate agreements that take the characteristics of the unit into account are made with every unit. It will be clear that such a *fine-tuning* will push the boundaries of the possible – you cannot have endless differences between units. And this is only one issue, and a simple one at that. In an organisation there are dozens of issues. Opt for fine-tuning in order to do justice to variety and the result will be a forest of interventions that it will be difficult to keep track of and manage.

Reinterpretation of the intervention changes it

A third obstacle is that in a very diverse network interventions are often distorted or reinterpreted. Different actors can interpret the same intervention differently.

Suppose the board of a university doesn't opt for tailor-made interventions and instead provides generic instructions with which the faculties and departments must comply. The faculties, for example, are obliged to carry out more fundamental research instead of applied research. This instruction will be interpreted differently by the different parties within the organisation. A faculty of business administration's definition of 'fundamental research' will be different to that of a faculty of theoretical physics. What the business studies faculty calls fundamental research, a theoretical physics faculty will probable consider to be a form of applied research. The business studies faculty will argue that fundamental research in the business studies field is very different than fundamental research in theoretical physics. The managers of the faculties concerned will pass their different definitions on to the different research groups within their faculties, which will all, once again, go through a process of reinterpretation. In this way the board's interventions will undergo a continuous process of reinterpretation, with the risk that in the end they will have no impact.

In a network there isn't only diversity, there are also interdependencies. Which barriers to decision-making and change do interdependencies throw up?

Hit-and-run is tempting, and will create chaos

Parties that are insufficiently aware of the interdependencies in a network could be tempted to exploit other parties at times when these other parties are dependent. Exploiting these other parties could, for example, mean approaching them aggressively and putting them under enormous pressure to vote for a decision. We call this the *hit-and-run* strategy: The time when others are dependent is the time at which you seize your opportunity by intervening aggressively (hitting), and then you try to get away from the other actors so you are not confronted with the consequences of your aggressive behaviour (running). Of course it isn't that simple. Interdependencies mean that the party that used the hit-and-run strategy will cross paths with the other parties again at sometimes unpredictable moments and can then be very dependent on these parties.

It will be clear that hit-and-run can work against the actor concerned: The other parties can see it as legitimization to extract their pound of flesh in an opportunistic manner. When several parties follow a hit-and-run strategy, this can lead to havoc in a network. An actor opts for hit and run, another actor hits back, and that increases the complexity of the decision-making.

Confusion and sluggishness

A party that is very aware of all the interdependencies can ascertain which other parties it is dependent on in order to take these dependencies into account as much as possible. The entirety of interdependencies can, however, be very confusing because the different types of interdependencies can manifest themselves at the same time. Actors can, for example, be dependent on each other for the achievement of their goals asynchronously, multilaterally and variably.

Such confusion can have a crippling effect. Actors need a lot of time to discover the other actors' positions, and a considerable amount of consultation is required because getting the other actors moving is difficult. The result could be the further complication of the decision-making.

Poor decision-making content

A third barrier inherent to interdependencies is that they lead to poor decision-making content. The decision-making is, to a great extent, the result of the balance of power in a network. When justice must be done to many different interests, there is a chance that the result is a dull compromise about which none of the parties is enthusiastic. A renowned architect can create a beautiful design for a cathedral. When this architect is dependent on local residents, financiers, municipal services and the future users and has to negotiate with these parties, there's a chance that very little of the splendour will remain. The tower must be shortened to appease the local residents, the amount of ornamentation is reduced to satisfy the financiers, the entrance must be smaller according to the municipality, and the future worshippers want a more traditional interior.

Opportunities

Variety offers opportunities for an intervening actor.

A higher probability of hitting the target with a portion of the parties

Diversity means that every actor in a network responds to a different kind of intervention: Actor A is responsive to intervention X, actor B to intervention Y, etc. So, in a situation with a lot of diversity, there is a greater chance that at least one or a few of the actors will be responsive to an intervention. Variety increases the chance that an actor's intervention will succeed with at least a portion of the parties.

An intervening actor has a number of strategies available to him to utilise this fact.

The first is that the intervening actor is satisfied with the fact that only a limited number of actors have responded to his intervention. Some problems only require some of the involved actors changing their behaviour for these problems to be solved. Traffic jam problems can be solved by only a few percent of the total number of drivers changing their behaviour. There is then no need for the other drivers to amend their behaviour.

The second strategy is that an actor instigates an intervention from which he can learn which parties will respond and which will not. He can then shape a follow-up intervention in a way that is likely to be more successful. For example, a minister of the environment learns from the first environmental agreements that some manufacturing processes offer many possibilities for environmental improvements and others offer very few possibilities. They can take this into account in a following intervention, for example, by differentiating between these two types of processes in the agreements.

This learning can, in the third place, also relate to the relationships between the parties in a network. Sometimes it is apparent that certain parties in a network have a lot of influence over other parties. Certain sectors have clear market leaders: If these companies change their behaviour, the other parties in the relevant network will often follow suit as a matter of course. This mechanism can be described using the biotechnology sector. When four or five large companies introduce an innovation, the other (80 to 90) companies follow virtually automatically. Such a mechanism offers opportunities for indirect change: By influencing the market leader, the behaviour of the other actors is also changed indirectly. In some manufacturing chains the link at the back of the chain appears to possess a lot of power. This too offers possibilities for indirect change. Whoever wins this link can steer the chain as a whole. Another reason this strategy is attractive is that the actor can concentrate on just a few key figures in the network.

Divide and conquer

The greater the variety in a network, the less the cooperation between the parties in the network goes without saying. This can have advantages for an intervening actor as it makes orchestrating a campaign against his intervention difficult. The top managers in an organisation with a lot of diversity can, thanks to this diversity, sometimes even intervene hierarchically, because blocking the intervention demands a degree of orchestration that is almost impossible for the different actors in a pluriform organisation to acheive. An intervening actor can utilise this: The diversity of the network can be used for a divide-and-conquer strategy.

Reinterpretation: constructive ambiguity

The process of reinterpretation, as described above – with the example of the two faculties and their different definitions of fundamental research – can also have a positive connotation: Parties interpret an intervention in such a way that it becomes more effective than its original sense. It is because the faculties reinterpreted the board's intervention and applied it to their own situation that the intervention was effective. Every faculty management has its own definition of 'fundamental research' that takes the characteristics of its own faculty's field of expertise into account. An intervening actor can once again utilise this fact by accepting that a term such as 'fundamental research' does not have an unambiguous meaning. On the contrary, it is ambiguous so can be interpreted differently per area of expertise. The board could therefore offer room for reinterpretation in the knowledge that, because of the reinterpretation, the intervention will be effective. The faculties will all make a shift to more fundamental research but in their own way and based upon their own definition of fundamental research. The definition of fundamental research is ambiguous, but it is a *constructive ambiguity*: By not formulating the goal of an intervention unambiguously and instead accepting the ambiguous character of the intervention, the intervention becomes effective.

Opportunities through interdependency

Interdependencies also offer an intervening actor opportunities.

Incentive for moderate behaviour

The first opportunity offered by interdependencies is that they force parties to behave moderately towards each other. When parties are dependent on each other, they must, to a certain extent, cooperate with each other. They will meet each other repeatedly, and the dependencies between them will change every time. Moderate behaviour could imply that it would not be sensible for a party to disregard another party or refuse to concede anything to this other party. This offers opportunities to an intervening actor: Others know they are dependent on him and will, therefore, concede to at least some of his wishes.

Increased complexity means more possibilities for exchange

A second opportunity is that complex interdependencies offer more chances for exchanges. When there are only a few interdependent parties and they are only dependent on each other for a few issues, the chance of a stalemate is greater than in a situation in which many parties are dependent on each other for many issues.

Content enrichment

A third chance is that interdependencies could lead to the content of the decision-making being enriched. When different parties with different interests and types of expertise sit around the table, there is a possibility that the decision they eventually make will be richer and will have more content than a decision made by one single actor. The architect who wants to build a beautiful theatre may be confronted with many parties that are in part opposed to the theatre – local residents, financiers, the municipal authorities and the users. Together these stakeholders could make it very difficult for the architect. But there is another picture: Thanks to the input of these parties, the theatre can also become more beautiful. Thanks to the local residents, it may perhaps fit in better in the neighbourhood. The financier suggests ways the theatre could also be used for other purposes and generate more revenue. The municipality promises a number of interventions in the area so that the theatre will come into its own more. And thanks to the users, the architect brings in a number of changes that will make the theatre more attractive for visitors.

What doesn't work: command and control, management by expertise and project management

At the end of this chapter we're going back to the dancing table. What are the consequences if one of the actors in a network isn't aware that he is in a network of interdependencies? Instead, he thinks it's a hierarchy. Take an actor, for example, who has a preference for corner C.

This actor could decide to adopt a command and control management style – that is the style that fits with a hierarchy. It will be clear that this will not be helpful; it will only increase the resistance.

The actor could be of the opinion that the question regarding the corner in which the table should end up is a structured problem. The experts he has hired have produced an analysis, the outcome of which is that the best place for the table is corner C. So the actor also opts for management by expertise. But, alas, the problem is unstructured; other parties have hired other experts who have come to other conclusions. When problems are unstructured, expertise content does not determine direction.

The actor could decide to apply the tools of the project management school. Suppose he has followed a project management course and has decided to apply all the lessons he has learned to the process in order to get the table to where he wants it to be. What did he learn during the course? His handbook contains a number of clear instructions:

- He must formulate explicit goals and communicate them clearly. So, he does this and states he wants to push the table into corner C.
- He must set a clear deadline for the achievement of his goals, so he states that the table must be in corner C on t3.

What happens to the dancing table if he actually carries out these recommendations? Formulating his explicit goal means the other parties know where he wants the table to be. They can use this knowledge to strengthen their own position in the process. But, the actor who prefers corner C does not yet know what the other parties want to do with the table, so he is not in a position to use the others for his own purposes.

The announcement about the deadline could incite parties to implement delaying tactics. Now the parties know the actor wants the table in corner C on t3, they could pull harder on the table because they have a preference for corner A. In this way they can reduce the actor's chance of success. They could block corner C by putting an obstacle in the table's way if it starts moving in that direction. They know their opponent has a deadline, so making an effort to keep the table out of corner C until then will be worthwhile. Not setting a deadline may have made it easier. In a nutshell: Project management in a network is not effective. It is counterproductive and works against the actor's interests. True, he has influence over the table's route through the room but not in the way he thought, and the route is still just as erratic.

And so at the end of this chapter we know what does not work in a network: command and control, management by expertise and project management. We also know that the features of a network provide barriers to decision-making and change as well as opportunities. In the following chapters we discuss which strategies, given these chances, will work.

2 Srategies for making decisions in networks

The process

What doesn't work – and what does

The question that now arises is how can the actors in these networks achieve collective decision-making? We know what doesn't work: command and control, management by expertise and project management. In this and the following chapter we will describe five key strategies that form the core of governance in networks.

The first essential strategy is, naturally, knowledge about the actors who together form the network, which means *actor analyses* are important. Understanding who the actors are and how they behave is at least as important as understanding the content of the problem.

The second is, it's not just the individual actors themselves who are important but also the relationships between the actors. *Maintenance and development of relationships* are important tools for influencing actors and decision-making.

Finally, anyone who wants to achieve anything in a network, with its erratic and unstructured decision-making, will have to cooperate with the other actors. In view of actors' differing interests, paying explicit attention to the way the cooperation process is organised and managed – the 'process management' – is essential.

These three strategies have little to do with the content. They relate to the 'who' factor (actors and their relationships) in the cooperation process that must be managed. There are also strategies whereby the content of a problem and solutions play a more central role. These will be discussed in Chapter 3.

Actors and actor analyses

It will be clear that decision-making in networks demands paying attention to the actors whose interests can be affected by the decision-making.

All actors in a network will want to know which of the other actors they need in order for a decision to be reached – they will make an actor analysis. What information do you need to know about these actors? And how simple or difficult will it be to gather this information?

At a minimum an actor analysis must always answer the following questions.

Question 1: Which actors' support is necessary in order to reach a decision, and what are these actors' opinions?

Let's go back to the example of the dancing table. If an actor wants the table to end up in corner A, this actor must assess which other actors are needed in order to achieve that goal. Towards this end, the actor must know which actors are relevant and which corner these actors think the table should end up in.

Although this kind of actor analysis may appear simple. it is far from it because why should the other actors tell someone else what they think? Would it be sensible for an actor who is against corner A to tell other actors that he wants the table in corner B? That is strategically important information not to be given away just like that. We'll come back to this later.

Question 2: What are these actors' interests?

Actors have standpoints. These standpoints are dictated by underlying interests. The difference between a standpoint and an interest is often illustrated with the example of an orange. Suppose that two parties are in conflict over an orange: Both parties want the orange and both parties are dependent on each other, so both parties must negotiate. The statement 'I want the orange' is a standpoint. This is followed by question as to what the parties' underlying interests are: *Why* are they adopting this standpoint; *why* do they want the orange? It's quite conceivable that one party wants to use the orange to make orange juice, while the other party wants the orange so the peel can be used to make skin care products.

Knowing not only the standpoint of the other party but also his underlying interest gives an actor room to negotiate. As long as the discussion is carried out at the standpoint level, there is little room for negotiation: Both parties want the same orange, and there's a good chance the orange will end up being cut in half. However, when the discussion is carried out at the underlying interest level, room to negotiate is created. In view of the different interests, it is obvious that one party should get the orange flesh from which to make orange juice and the other party should get the peel to make skin care products.

Question 3: What are these actors' resources?

The influence an actor can exercise in order to achieve his own interests is, to a great extent, determined by his power sources. Power sources can be factors such as money, judicial authority, knowledge, relationships and reputation.

One important aspect in this respect is the difference between production power and blockade power (Coleman, 1971). Production power means that an actor can make a positive contribution towards the achievement of something –

can contribute towards the 'production' of a decision. A finance minister and a chief financial officer (CFO) have production power: They can make budgets available that will, for example, enable a positive decision to be made regarding a project. Blockade power means that an actor can only impede something. Many protest movements, in particular, are said to have blockade power. They may have the resources to stop a project but often are not the sources to realise something. In large organisations, people often complain that staff departments (Legal primarily) have this blockade power – they can stop projects but do not realise anything themselves – only the business units can do so.

A party can also have a diffused power position, which makes it unclear to the other parties what that actor's actual power position is. What power sources that party has may not be clear. A diffused position can also stem from the fact that, although parties have power sources at their disposal, whether or not they will utilise them is not clear. Some resources are, due to their nature, always diffuse. Reputation is a resource that, by nature, can never be precisely measured or precisely expressed as a unit.

The combination of actors and resources can be used to arrive at a typology of actors. Suppose that a party wants to make a particular decision and depends on other actors. The first question is: What are these other actors' opinions and interests? Three options are possible:

- An actor supports the decision and sides with the pro camp;
- An actor is against the decision and joins the anti-camp; or
- An actor opts for the 'keep one's options open' strategy (Lubben, 2015): At this stage the actor is expressing no preferences, opting instead to be a *fence-sitter.*

The next question is: What resources do each of these actors have, and what type of power does this lead to – production power, blockade power or a more diffuse power position? This results in Table 2.1.

An actor analysis is more than an analysis

Although carrying out an actor analysis (Burandt, Gralla, & John, 2015; Enserink et al., 2010) may sound like a simple, analytical activity, it often

Table 2.1 Typology of actors

	Support	*Oppose*	*Keep options open*
Production power			
Blockade power			
Diffuse power position			

isn't. Suppose a highway agency wants to build a new road alongside a nature reserve. If there's a lot of opposition to the plan from local communities, environmental groups and local authorities, the highway agency will probably carry out or commission an actor analysis. The following problems could, however, arise:

- *An actor analysis is strategic information.* Why would other actors reveal their opinions, interests and resources? That is strategically important information the highway agency can use to strengthen its own network position.
- *There is dissent regarding the actor analysis.* An actor can have certain views regarding his own opinions, interests and resources, but what if the other actors don't share his views? What if one actor in a network thinks he or she has a good reputation and many relationship networks, but the other actors think this is totally not the case?
- *There are uncertainties regarding the actor analysis.* In a number of cases the actors' opinions, interests and resources are not clear or not yet clear. Perhaps at this point in time they still haven't determined their position, and perhaps as yet they don't even know what interest they have in a specific issue.
- *The actor analysis doesn't take dynamics into account.* Parties' opinions, interests and resources may change over time. An opinion held today may change tomorrow, for example, if new information becomes available.
- *Having resources and using resources are two different things.* An actor may have certain resources – and a lot of power – but what does that say? The real question is whether the actor is prepared to use these resources. Answering this question in advance is often very difficult.

How to deal with these problems

In the first place an actor analysis can be carried out using the reputation method: The analyst not only asks actors about their own opinions, interests and values, the analyst also asks them about their views regarding the opinions, interests and values of others. Put another way, you ask about the reputations of the other actors.

The outcome is that for each actor you have both a self-image and the image that other parties have of this actor. When these images converge, there's a good chance that the analyst has a correct understanding of the actor. When they diverge, there's a good chance this is not the case. This, by the way, is not absolutely certain – even in converging images, reality can be other.

There's another reason why the reputation method is interesting. Suppose that actor A holds a strong power position in a network because this actor has a lot of resources. Thanks to the reputation method, the analyst learns that other actors have a totally different perception of actor A. They see actor A as a weak actor with very little power. The conclusion must be that either A has a very wrong self-image or that the other actors are completely mistaken regarding actor A's reputation. But there's more: The perception of the other actors will probably have a considerable influence on their behaviour.

They consider actor A to be a weak party and will adjust their strategy on the basis of this assumption. That could be a mistake – it could make the decision-making process even more erratic. Divergent perceptions regarding actors' positions say something about the factual correctness of perceptions but also about the behaviour that will be evoked by these perceptions – and about the risks the decision-making process may encounter as a result.

In the second place it is important to be aware that the distinction between analysis and actions is not clear-cut. The simple thought could be that first an analyst carries out an actor analysis, and then, based on this analysis, actors determine their actions and strategies in the decision-making process. But it's never that simple.

During the analysis, actors will already be behaving strategically. They know that the information they provide regarding their own standpoints, interests and resources (or, via the reputation method, regarding the standpoints, interests and resources of other actors) will be used in the decision-making process, so providing the information is not an attractive proposition for them. They could even decide to provide misinformation – that could certainly give them a strategic advantage. This means analysis and action are intertwined and cannot be separated cleanly. An actor analysis is not only an analysis, it is also a strategy in the decision-making game. This is why, in many cases, producing a very detailed actor analysis makes very little sense. An actor analysis is a strategy – so the question about what makes the perfect actor analysis is perhaps less interesting than the question of how an actor analysis can be used strategically.

In the third place, as soon as the decision-making starts and actors take their first actions, a new reality is created. Actors will review their positions and, therefore, their standpoints and answers to the question as to whether or not they will utilise their resources.

This means that a sequence of analysis then action will never happen. An actor analysis is a continuous process that takes place not only prior to the decision-making process but also during it.

Relationships and relationship management: redundancy

Their relationship network is an important tool for actors. The more relationships an actor has, the more possibilities for acquiring the support of other actors. Relationships have at least two functions: They are advantageous for actors when it comes to acquiring information, and they can also strengthen strategic positions within a network.

Types of relationship

The relationships an actor maintains can by typed in two ways:

- Functional and nonfunctional relationships: Functional relationships have a clear significance for an actor. Actors cannot carry out their core tasks without having these types of relationships. Nonfunctional relationships conversely have no direct significance for an actor's core tasks. For example, the relationship network an environmental inspectorate (the organisation that maintains certain environmental legislation) maintains with businesses is functional; any relationships it has with archaeology clubs are nonfunctional.

- Strong and weak relationships ('*strong ties*' and '*weak ties*' [Granovetter, 1973; Todo, Matous, & Inoue, 2016; Zenou, 2015]): Strong relationships or ties are relationships that are used intensively. Weak relationships or ties are relationships that are maintained for incidental use. The inspectorate mentioned above can maintain strong relationships with the environment minister and *weak ties* with, for example, a university faculty in which environmental research is carried out.

Relationship formation often has a pragmatic connotation: Actors enter into relationships with parties they need. From a pragmatic point of view, there can be a strong bias towards developing primarily functional and strong relationships.

The now classic Granovetter research (Granovetter, 1973) does show, however, that weak relationships and nonfunctional ties can be very important for an actor's network position. Networks are always dynamic. Actors' positions can change, and they can become more important than they were previously. New actors can join the network, which constantly makes new problems and solutions available. These dynamics mean that the actor who today plays a marginal role in a network could, tomorrow, occupy a central position. *Weak ties* with this actor could, in this case, suddenly become very important. When the custodian of a fourteenth century castle complains about damage due to the polluting activities of an adjacent industry, the environmental inspectorate's relationship with the archaeology club suddenly becomes very valuable. When a conflict arises regarding the environmental effects of certain manufacturing processes, its relationships with the university are useful, for example, because the university in question is carrying out authoritative research into the environmental effects of this kind of manufacturing process.

When actors maintain these four types of relationship with a multitude of actors, we call this a redundant relationship network: They maintain long-lasting relationships with other actors, even at times when this does not appear to be useful (nonfunctional), and pay explicit attention to *weak ties*. Redundant sometimes has a negative connotation – superfluous to requirements or a waste of energy. Here it is meant positively – backup (Bendor, 1985).

Before we discuss these two advantages, let's make sure there is no confusion regarding our use of the term 'networks'. In this book when we talk about 'networks', we mean an entirety of interdependent relationships. When an actor is in a network he is, therefore, dependent on others for the achievement of his goals.

The term 'network' can, however, have another meaning: the entirety of relationships maintained by an actor. In that case we are not talking about an actor who is *in* a network but about an actor who *has* a network.

Because these two definitions of 'network' can lead to confusion, in this book we talk about 'redundant relationships' when we mean this second definition. For the rest both meanings of 'network' have everything to do with each other. An actor who is in a network (as a pattern of interdependencies) needs to have networks (redundant relationships) to service his or her own interests and to have an impact on decision-making.

Redundant relationships and information

The first advantage gained by an actor who has his relationship management well organised is a stronger information position.

A lot of information, both content related and strategic

A redundant relationship network gives actors many channels through which they can receive information. Some of the information an actor receives is content related: information about the nature of problems, the available solutions, comparable problems and solutions elsewhere, etc. Some of the information an actor receives is strategy related: information about the positions and perceptions of parties, the extent to which they are able to cooperate and the conditions under which they are prepared to cooperate. The better an actor's information in this respect, the more chance this actor has of taking the right action at the right time.

Checking and double-checking information

Redundancy also means that an actor can receive information about the same subject via several channels. This is very important because actors in a network behave strategically, which includes disseminating information strategically. This can mean that an actor only provides other parties with information that strengthens his own position. The time at which information is disseminated can also be of strategic importance.

In view of this strategic behaviour, an actor who is dependent on only one relationship – one source – for his information runs a major risk: Either this actor doesn't have information that is available to other actors, or this actor receives information that, due to its one-sided bias, cannot be verified or put into perspective. However, if actors receive information from several sources, they are able to *check and double-check* the information. They can arrange, compare and critically question the information they have received via the different relationships and, therefore, use it in a more intelligent way.

'By chance' information

This system of redundant relationships also increases the likelihood that an actor will receive 'by chance' information that can be used to reach a solution to a problem. 'Chance' plays a major role in decision-making in networks. When many actors are involved in decision-making, each of whom is the owner of particular problems and particular solutions, the chance of unexpected opportunities or occurrences increases, and problems and solutions can, by chance, become linked in very surprising ways.

So, the more relationships an actor maintains, the greater the likelihood that he can use the unexpected opportunity or occurrence. What these opportunities or occurrences will be is often impossible to forecast. What looks like pure chance or a fluke is, in fact, enforced luck: He who maintains relationships with many parties knows that many unforeseen opportunities come along.

Repertoire-building

Information only has value if it has meaning. Redundant Frelationships can be used for *repertoire-building* (Schön, 1983, p.315), the acquiring of experience that could later play a role in the interpretation of new information. The more relationships an actor maintains, the more varied the types of experience the actor gains. This creates a reference framework that offers the possibility of giving meaning to a multitude of pieces of information. An actor with a repertoire of experiences at his disposal will find it relatively easy to assess the significance of new information. An actor capable of doing this combines the best effects of redundancy: He receives a lot of information, which gives him a high degree of problem-solving capability and, at the same time, increases his ability to interpret the information.

Redundant relationships and power

A redundant pattern of relationships also gives an actor a number of strategic advantages: It strengthens his position in a network.

Room to manoeuvre

Redundant relationships give an actor in a network room to manoeuvre. The person who maintains many relationships always has a fallback position: If one actor won't support his initiative, he can fall back on another actor with whom he also maintains a relationship. This is an example of *multiple sourcing*: An actor ensures that for certain activities he is not dependent on just one other actor.

For an example from a very different world, in his book *Diplomacy* former US. Henry Kissinger analyses the strategic behaviour of Prussian Chancellor Otto von Bismarck. In the nineteenth century Europe was a patchwork of states and mini-states. Prussia developed alliances and maintained relationships in every direction. This created a pattern of some overlapping and some competing alliances that were often also interconnected. The result of this was the creation of an entirety of relationships so complex that 'Prussia would always be closer to each of the contending parties than they were to one another" (Kissinger, 1994, p.122). Prussia was always around and because of this acquired considerable power and scope.

At first glance this entirety of relationships looks chaotic: a spaghetti-like structure of countless intertwined relationships. In practice this spaghetti is an actor's strength: the greater the number of relationships, the more room to manoeuvre, and perhaps the less room to manoeuvre for the others.

Less predictability

Closely linked to this is the fact that redundant relationships make an actor's behaviour less predictable. It is difficult for the other actors to assess how the actor with the redundant relationships – in the example above, von Bismarck – will behave. An actor with many relationships always has a fallback position. If actor A negotiates with actor B and actor B has redundant relationships, there is a chance that actor B will try to exert influence on actor A via actor C. In a network predictability can be a major strategic disadvantage. It is also easier for other actors to tune their behaviour to that of a predictable party than to a party that is moving (Rhodes, 1991, p.530). Unpredictability will make the other parties more cautious.

Redundancy makes an actor attractive

An actor with redundant relationships is an attractive partner for the other parties in a network. This actor can function as an access portal to others and to the sources and information of these others. As we said earlier, actors can have both strong and weak ties at their disposal. The more relationships, the more attractive they are – and the advantage of weak ties is that maintaining this type of relationship often costs an actor very little. This enables him to maintain a lot of relationships of this type, which can make him an interesting ally.

Redundancy forces other actors to moderate their behaviour

Finally, an important consequence of what has been discussed is that other parties will often moderate their behaviour towards the actor with redundant relationships. The fact that others will meet this actor in a number of decision-making processes because of the redundant relationships will incentivize them to behave modestly and cooperatively. Being brusque with the actor concerned in respect of issue A in network X could work against them when they meet the same actor in respect to issue B in network Y. The more relationships an actor has, the greater the chance of this kind of meeting and thus the greater the incentive for moderate behaviour.

Two warnings

All of this leads us to give two warnings. In the first place there is a major paradox. Actors with many relationships at their disposal are potentially powerful, but they will often use these relationships to a limited extent. Using the redundant relationships in your own favour increases the chances that relationships get damaged. A relationship is two-sided: For both parties it is important to maintain the relationship – which is not the case if one of those parties is constantly utilising the relationship in its own favour. Therefore, the actor who maintains redundant relationships will find that, on the one hand, there are many opportunities, but on the other hand, there's a dependency on others. As the saying goes, 'The spider in the web can also become the fly in the web'.

This came very clearly to the fore in our research into the failure of the commercial sports broadcaster Sport 7 in the Netherlands. Sport 7 was established by a consortium that included two large companies (Philips and telecom operator KPN) as well as the national football association. Philips and KPN had good relationships with the Dutch government. This made them very attractive to the other consortium partners because Sport 7 needed the Dutch government's support at several points in time. However, because Philips and KPN had such good relationships, they had to behave moderately. Philips and KPN needed the Dutch government not only for Sport 7 but also for numerous other issues. After the downfall of Sport 7, one of the other (disappointed) shareholders observed that Philips and KPN yielded to political pressure and political resistance to the sports broadcaster. Both companies may have had many relationships, but they couldn't always use them as they wished (Bruijn, Heuvelhof, & Kuit, 1999, p.102).

In the second place it is also necessary for an actor's strategic position that the other actors consider this actor a reliable partner. Actors who constantly use all the possibilities offered by their relationship network lose their trustworthiness. Actors with many relationships who constantly use the room to manoeuvre make themselves unpredictable and can be perceived as untrustworthy. Actors who are untrustworthy can lose their power position. That leads to the power paradox: The more power you have, the greater the necessity to use it in moderation – to use your power position as little as possible. The question of how the strategies in this chapter relate to the need for trustworthiness will be dealt with later in this book.

Process management

Where are we now? There are problems that demand decision-making. These problems must, however, be solved within a network of interdependencies. They are unstructured and, on top of that, dynamic rather than stable. The decision-making processes related to this type of problem will therefore always be erratic and unstructured – see the example of the dancing table.

Suppose now that in that network with its erratic decision-making there is a party who wants to achieve something. The party concerned has a problem he wants to solve, but to do so, he needs the support of other parties. However, these parties will not give their support as a matter of course because they have other interests and standpoints.

Chapter 1 describes what doesn't work

- Command and control means that someone imposes their unilateral decision on others. In reality a decision is reached in a process of interaction between the involved actors.
- Management by expertise means that the experts in the content field determine what the problem is and its solution. In reality THE problem and THE solution don't exist, and problems and solutions can only be determined in a process of interaction.
- Project management means that a decision-making process can be totally planned. In reality it can't – decision-making is a process not a project.

That's three times that decision-making is shown to be a process of interaction among involved parties. This makes decision-making in a network dependent to a great extent on the management of this process – on the process management (Bruijn, Heuvelhof, & Veld, 2010).

Suppose once again that in a network of interdependencies there is a highway agency that really wants to build a bridge over a canal because it could solve the region's congestion problems. However, there are a lot of other parties that aren't keen on the idea. Local municipalities are against it, the environmental movement is against it, the inland waterways authority is against it, and the regional authority, which must cofinance the bridge, also has its doubts.

The solution to this problem demands focusing on the actors: What are their standpoints, interests and resources? Redundant relationships are an important tool for the highway agency in its endeavour to achieve its goals.

The highway agency knows one thing for sure in advance: The decision-making process will be erratic and unstructured. And if the other actors also have redundant relationships and use them, the decision-making will be even more erratic and could go on forever. Think back to the dancing table, to all the pushing and pulling that will go on and on without any satisfactory outcome for the involved actors. Even if the table does end up in a corner, there are actors who have an interest in getting it out of the corner again, and so the pushing-and-pulling party will continue.

Endless pushing and pulling is unattractive, not only for the highway agency but also for the other actors. A decision-making process that goes on forever costs these actors a lot of energy. Maybe they also have an interest in a decision. Some of them want the decision to be that there won't be a bridge. Some want the decision to be that there will be a ferry. Others may be for a bridge but only if it's a toll bridge. But all of them would have problems with being involved in an endless decision-making process.

How can the highway agency manage such a chaotic process? How can it play the role of process manager? Such a chaotic environment will often generate a need for some stability and predictability among the actors. Hardly anybody has an interest in chaos. So, how do you create a degree of stability and predictability? The essence of the answer to this question is extraordinarily simple: Involve actors in the decision-making process by making it attractive for them. A decision-making process is attractive for other actors if it complies with four core demands (Bruijn, Heuvelhof, & Veld, 2010).

Openness

A process is attractive if an actor doesn't try to make unilateral decisions but rather adopts an open attitude. Other parties are given the opportunity to share in steering the decision-making and can, therefore, also say what issues are of interest to them and should be on the agenda. In the example of the highway agency, they must involve the parties with an interest in the bridge in the decision-making and give them the chance to influence the decision to be made. The highway agency will invite them to be involved in the decision-making and also ask them which issues they would like to be put on the agenda. Openness, therefore, relates to both the question of who is involved and the agenda for the decision-making.

Protecting core values

Openness isn't always attractive for the parties invited to participate in a process. Everyone injects their own interests, which means every party risks having insufficient ability to achieve their own interests. The consequence can be that the result at the end of the process is unsatisfactory for one or more parties while at the same time it is difficult for them to still withdraw from the process. This is why one criterion for a good process is that it protects the core values of the parties (Duh, Belak, & Milfelner, 2010). Perhaps they have to accept some compromises; they'll never be able to achieve all their interests, but their core values are protected.

A key core value for the environmental movement is that the quality of the environment should not deteriorate. Suppose that the environmental movement is against the bridge because it will mean more traffic along some roads that run alongside a nature preserve. The outcome of the decision-making process could be that the bridge will be built, but the speed limit on the roads alongside the nature preserve will be lowered and that environmental compensatory measures will be implemented in other areas. On balance the environment is better off. But now suppose this is not the case – on balance the environment is worse off. As that goes against one of the environmental movement's core values, they must be given the space to oppose the decision, even if they were involved in reaching that decision. If you, as an environmental movement, know from before the process begins that you will not be bound to the outcome if it infringes upon your core values, you will be more relaxed during the decision-making process. The process will be safer and, as a result, will progress more smoothly.

Incentives for progress

An open process in which all, or many, parties participate and in which parties are offered security through the protection of their core values has one major risk: There is a very good chance that there will be consultation and negotiation but no certainty that this will result in a decision being made. There is a chance that all that will be achieved is sluggish processes that never produce a clear result. This is why it is important to create the conditions that will ensure a steady speed and progress in the processes.

The most important incentive for progress is that the actors involved in the process have the idea that 'there is something in it for me' – if an actor participates and supports the decision that is made, he will benefit. In the following chapter we will describe how such a situation can be created through a 'multi-issue game', but we'll give you just a hint here. If the highway agency wants to make it attractive for the parties to not only participate but also reach a decision relatively quickly, the process must be about more than just the bridge. If the decision-making is about the bridge alone, it very quickly becomes an 'either/or' process – you're either for or against the bridge, so there's a fair chance of a stalemate. But what if the highway agency puts other issues on the agenda as well – not just the bridge but also the development of a nature preserve, the speed limit on the access roads, new agreements regarding maintenance by the region's business community or the development of new cycling paths? This agenda might make participation attractive for parties because they are very interested in, for example, an extra nature preserve and more cycling paths. If participation is attractive because there's something in it for different parties, they could also have an interest in fast decision-making.

Incentives for relevant content

So, parties can participate in an open decision-making process, their core values can be protected, and there should be incentives for making progress, but one risk of such a strong emphasis on the process of decision-making is that the content gets lost in the mire. The parties may reach agreement, but then it transpires that the content of their decision is debatable. This is why a good process offers enough guarantees regarding the quality of the decision-making content. Let's return to the example of the highway agency. Suppose that the actors in the process come to a deal. One component of the deal is that the existing nature preserve will be extended and additional cycling paths will be constructed. There is a chance that although the parties that participated in the process reached a consensus, the experts are not so happy with the plans. For example, they may point out that the cycling paths should be laid out differently so cyclists could enjoy the nature preserve more and have fewer problems with the vehicle traffic on the access roads. It is important that such experts also have a role in the process. A deal between parties can become overly political – that means the deal is good from a political point of view (for example because it keeps all the parties happy) – but keeping everyone happy could have decreased the quality of the content or even made it impossible to implement.

A process must always do right by these four components and is, therefore, always also a trade-off between these four components. A process without openness will be experienced as a disguised form of project management and command and control. A process in which the core values of parties are not protected is, for these parties, unattractive and unsafe. There is a very good chance that they will continuously delay the process due to their lack of trust or may even refuse en masse to participate. If there are no incentives for keeping the process moving, it will become sluggish and can lose its authority. Parties may drop out of it. If there are no facilities to create content and quality, the process can lead to poor results that are vulnerable to criticism from outside.

The importance of process agreements

The idea is, therefore, that decision-making will progress less erratically if it is based on these four principles. The four principles can be translated into agreements the parties reach regarding the manner in which the process will proceed. Examples of process agreements are:

- *Agreements about entry and exit:* The process agreements related to entry and exit specify which parties are participating in the decision-making and the conditions under which parties may enter or exit the process.
- *Agreements related to the decision-making:* These agreements specify how parties reach decisions: for example, by consensus or by a majority of votes. Further regulations regarding the way losing minorities are handled could also be agreed.
- *Agreements related to conflict management:* These agreements concern the way conflicts are settled – by voting, by transferring the conflict to another body, through arbitration, etc.
- *Agreements related to the organisation of the process:* These are agreements regarding the way in which the decision-making is organised. For example, is there a steering group, are there working groups, and is there perhaps a group that monitors the quality and progress of the decision-making? Sometimes agreements must also be made about the chairmanship and management of these groups and the decision-making process.
- *Agreements related to the planning and budget:* The planning describes which activities will be carried out during the process, in which order and

by what deadlines. The planning also includes an estimate of the costs of the activities and the process management and specifies who will be accountable for which costs.

These are only examples. The parties can, of course, come to an agreement about other aspects of the process. What is important for making process agreements acceptable to and plausible for the involved actors is that their contents are neutral. These types of agreements only work if they are not *biased* in favour of or against certain content-related solutions.

Process agreements can be more or less formal. Sometimes they are unwritten rules that are adhered to by the parties more or less intuitively. Sometimes they are written rules, which are sometimes the result of negotiation. This is regularly the case in the diplomatic world: There is a content-related conflict; the parties know they need each other for a solution to this conflict and that they must formulate process agreements for the negotiations. These process agreements can have a major influence on the decision-making, so the first negotiations are related to the process agreements.

Finally, there is the question of who manages the process: Who will take on the role of process manager, the actor who supervises compliance with the process agreements, manages the process and facilitates the decision-making?

The process manager must, of course, be independent and must not favour any of the parties. Although, for this reason, in some projects an independent third party is asked to fulfil the role of process manager, it can also be fulfilled by one of the involved parties. Having an involved party as process manager rather than a third party can be advantageous – an involved party has a greater knowledge of the other actors and of the issues on the agenda. The party that initiated the decision-making is a candidate for the function of process manager as it is the largest party that commands the most resources.

There are, therefore, plenty of options. The most important criterion here is the views of the parties involved in the process. There is no right or wrong answer; it all depends on the opinions of the parties. A process manager must have the support of all the parties, so the judgement of the parties regarding who should take on the role of process manager is the deciding factor when it comes to making a choice.

3 Strategies for making decisions in networks

The content

From who to what

The strategies discussed in the previous chapter had little to do with the content. The identification of actors, the utilisation of relationships and the management of the process are highly actor-oriented strategies. They relate more to the 'who' than the 'what'.

In this chapter we are going to focus on a crucial strategy related to the content of the decision-making. A reminder: Problems are unstructured, which means that different parties can have very different opinions about the nature of a problem. You don't solve an unstructured problem by bringing in content-related expertise – an expert's opinions can almost always be open to debate. This does not, of course, mean that content and expertise don't matter in decision-making processes. The answers to certain questions, such as "How do you get a process started?" and "How do you make participation in a process attractive for parties?" do naturally have everything to do with the content.

Multi-issue games

A party in a network wants to achieve a project for which there is insufficient support from other parties. How will this party set to work? She will try to start a decision-making process with the other actors. But why should these other actors get involved? They're against the project, so what could they gain by participating in the decision-making? And, if they participate, why should they be cooperative? They are against the project, so there's a likelihood they will do everything they can to block the decision-making related to it.

This can be formulated more concisely: When the party who wants to achieve the project talks solely about the project, it's very probable the decision-making will come to nothing. It's a one-issue game: There is only one item on the agenda – the project. A one-issue game always leads to *either/or* decision-making. The others are either for or against the project, and there's a chance that the gap between the proponents and opponents will only increase over time.

That's why in this sort of situation it's important to change the agenda: to turn the one-issue agenda into a multi-issue agenda and thus create a multi-issue decision-making process (Fatima, Wooldridge, & Jennings, 2006).

Example: a divided family

The essence of a multi-issue agenda and the resulting multi-issue decision-making process can best be explained using the example of a family that must decide where they are going for their summer holiday.

The family comprises five 'players' – a father, a mother, a daughter aged eighteen, a daughter aged sixteen and a son aged six. Both the father and mother have an income of fifty units, so they both have an important resource. From a managerial perspective this might be problematic: The financial resources are divided equally across two players, so there is a 'distributed power' situation. If the father had an income of zero and the mother an income of one hundred, the financial power would rest with one person and, from a managerial point of view, that would probably be simpler.

The elder daughter also has a power position – she is an adult and is therefore no longer subject to parental authority. She can block her parents' decisions, which gives her 'blockade power' – someone with blockade power can impede decisions but cannot create them. Her parents' financial means gives them 'production power' – they can create decisions.

Does the six-year-old son have power? Small players always have 'chaos power' – they can create chaos and thus force an issue. Perhaps he has learned that he can achieve a lot by lying in the middle of a train aisle and screaming! The prospect that he can create such chaos may cause his parents to become more indulgent at certain moments.

All the parties – including the small party – have relationship power. They maintain relationships with others and can activate these relationships. Maybe the two sisters adore their little brother and are inclined to support him in everything – certainly if a conflict with their father is involved. If such a conflict arises, this small player will probably activate these relationships, showing that his power is greater than his father initially thought.

Suppose the father wants to achieve a project. He wants to go on a family vacation this summer because he realises this may be the last time they all holiday together. With this in mind, he is prepared to spend more on the holiday than in previous years. He analyses the preferences of the family members, the costs of the different options, the destinations the family has already visited and arrives at the ideal holiday. This family is situated in Europe, and the father's favourite holiday destination is the East Coast of the United States. He wants to take the family there for three weeks in August.

Now he must gather support for this plan, but it seems nobody is enthusiastic about it. The mother does want to holiday as family but not on the US East Coast. The older daughter is still talking to her boyfriend about a summer holiday. The younger daughter does want to go to the East Coast of the USA but not with the whole family. And the six-year-old son doesn't express any opinion – for the time being he wants to keep his options open.

What we have here is a network: Many actors, with every actor having a power position and very different opinions. The content of the problem is unstructured – you can't say that the holiday in the US is the right solution to the problem. There are also dynamics involved – the elder daughter may be against it but for the time being is a participant in the decision-making. Her attitude may be different tomorrow if she and her boyfriend agree to have their own holiday – and then participating in the decision-making process on a family holiday will no longer be attractive to her.

The father is sitting with his head in his hands. Nobody supports his plan; nobody is making an effort to reach a decision about the holiday. The more he pressures the family members to agree to his project, the more opposition he encounters. What we have here is a one-issue agenda – there is only one item on the agenda and that leads to an either/or process: You are either for or against it, and this automatically results in a stalemate.

What's the way out? The father must make it a multi-issue process. This changing of the game is carried out in two phases:

- Formulate the problem is broad rather than narrow terms: Don't say that the problem is that the coming summer offers the last chance for a family holiday. Instead say, for example, that as a father you want to invest in the quality of the family's life in the coming year. A narrow problem formulation scares people off, a broad problem formulation generally doesn't.
- Invite the parties to suggest issues they think will contribute towards a high-quality family life: These should be included on the agenda. What could such issues be? Perhaps someone wants to talk about the layout of the rooms in the family's house, about having a pet, about making agreements for eating meals together, or about rules concerning going out or sharing chores. Naturally, the father puts the summer holiday on the agenda, and perhaps one family member thinks that this may be the time to put a skiing trip on the agenda as well. All kinds of other issues could also be added, such as mobile phones, trips, redecorating the house, a driver's license or a pocket-money increase.

Now we have a multi-issue agenda. One characteristic of such an agenda is that very often the added issues have very little to do with the original issue – the summer holiday – but have everything to do with the parties involved in the process. A good multi-issue agenda is one in which each of the involved parties can find several issues to which he or she is attracted and perhaps a few issues to which he or she is totally opposed. The younger daughter, for example, could be delighted that a new room layout, a skiing holiday or new going-out rules are up for discussion but could be totally against acquiring a family pet. This means there is potential 'gain and pain' for every party.

A multi-issue game contains a number of important incentives that are beneficial for the decision-making.

Incentive to participate in the process

In the first place, a multi-issue agenda is a strong incentive for actors to participate in the decision-making process. To use jargon: It makes use of the entry option. What will the elder daughter do if she receives an invitation to a family meeting with only one item on the agenda – the proposal to travel to the US? She would probably decline the invitation – there's nothing in it for her. And anyway she is an adult so not bound to decisions made by her parents. But now there's an invitation with a multi-issue agenda, including issues that could give her gain and others that could give her pain. That's a strong incentive to participate in the family meeting. If she doesn't, other people will talk about the issues and there's a chance they will come to a deal that could give her pain – and no gain.

What's important here is that this incentive for participation could also be a moral incentive. Suppose an environmental organisation refuses to participate in the decision-making related to a large infrastructure project. The environmental organisation is against this project but doesn't want to participate in the decision-making. There could be good reasons for this. By not participating you can prevent yourself from becoming a *captive* of the other parties in the decision-making process. Perhaps you can exert more influence on the decision-making if you are not sitting at the table because then it's easier for you to activate the media. But what if it's a multi-issue agenda during which other issues are going to be discussed, such as water quality, the extension of a national park and other environmental issues? At the least it will be more difficult for the environmental organisation to refuse to participate because these are issues that affect its core values. Refusing to participate despite this might cause it to face legitimacy problems – people could say that it is morally wrong not to sit down with the other parties because there are important environmental issues on the agenda. It is a moral obligation of environmentalists to defend these issues.

Incentive to continue participating

Perhaps the incentive to participate in the decision-making doesn't seem very important – you can, after all, also decide over time to withdraw from the decision-making. But it's not as simple as that. A party who has joined in the decision-making– has decided to sit down with the other parties – cannot just up and leave the process. There are two reasons for this:

- Anyone who leaves the process will see their profit evaporate and may end up with a loss. A family member who would welcome new, more flexible going-out rules, is totally against a pet but who leaves the process, naturally runs a major risk: no more flexible going-out rules plus now living with a family pet. The process offers the prospect of gain that is lost if a party utilises the exit option.

- Perhaps more important still: Anyone who leaves the process breaches the trust of the other parties and becomes untrustworthy. The two sisters in the family pull together and try to gain support for a skiing holiday. To do so, they need the support of just one more family member. And they succeed – the mother also supports the skiing holiday. Now one of the sisters decides to leave the process because she's dissatisfied with what she is getting out of it. That means the skiing holiday is once again uncertain – and this was a big deal for the other sister. She could now consider her exiting sister to be very untrustworthy. They've pulled together through family meeting after family meeting and invested in each other. The exiting sister knows how important skiing is for her sibling, yet now she's walked out of the process and left the other sister sitting there empty-handed. That is untrustworthy behaviour.

We will deal with the topic of trustworthiness in Chapter 7. Here we will observe that parties in a network meet each other continuously in relation to different issues. Their interdependency is recurring, so a party that is labelled as 'untrustworthy' is not an attractive partner for other parties. Anyone who behaves badly in a process by leaving it or damaging it in another way runs the risk of achieving less in other processes.

Incentive for depolarisation and for give and take

A one-issue agenda is a strong incentive for polarisation because it demands an either/or decision. The father is for the holiday; the others are against it. So, both sides will put forward arguments to support their point of view, and there is a good chance that the two sides will become more and more entrenched in their own opinion. There is also a risk that every action the father takes may be seen by the others as yet another underhand attempt to get the family to the East Coast of the United States. This is how a one-issue agenda can be a source of endless and fruitless discussions, conflicts and distrust. In other words, a one-issue agenda can polarise a family and lead to tense relationships.

By contrast, a multi-issue agenda forces parties to give and take. Everyone will understand – or learn during the process – that they have no chance of getting something they want if the others don't also get something. The process becomes one of give and take, of wanting each other to gain something, and that leads to depolarisation (Flinders & Buller, 2006), more relaxed attitudes and, as a result, better cooperation in the decision-making process.

Incentive for cooperative behaviour – coalitions vary

The family will devote several meetings to the multi-issue agenda. There will be consensus regarding some issues, but for other issues there will be family members for and family members against them. Mother and the two daughters are for the concept-agreement about the skiing holiday, the father and son are against. Father and the elder daughter are for having a pet, the others are against. Mother and younger daughter are for more flexible going-out rules. So is the son – he's too young to be interested for himself – but he's supporting his sister because he wants her support regarding another issue. Father and elder daughter are against relaxing the going-out rules.

What's happening here? For each issue there are different 'for' and 'against' coalitions. Variable coalitions lead to incentives for cooperative behaviour. Every player is confronted with the same situation: The person who is your opponent today regarding one issue is the person you need to work with tomorrow regarding another issue. Because you need that person tomorrow, you must behave moderately and cooperatively today. The multi-issue agenda creates dependencies, and when there are dependencies, cooperative behaviour pays.

Incentive for a learning process

A decision-making process with a multi-issue agenda (Flamini, 2007) can also be a strong incentive for learning on two levels.

First and foremost learning can take place on the power relationship level. The parties learn where the power relationships lie in the process and which options are achievable and which are unachievable. The younger daughter is very interested in a new room layout in the family house, but during the course of the decision-making process, she realises there is no support for this from any other family member. In this case it is probably sensible for her to save her energy for other issues she considers important and which she does have a chance of achieving.

Second, parties can learn about the content. Having a lot of issues on the agenda often makes interesting combinations possible. During a holiday on the US East Coast, one of the children could obtain a driver's license. There could be a decision to shorten the summer holiday, which would allow for a ski trip. All kinds of interesting combinations are possible that may be difficult to predict or imagine in advance. This means the parties have opportunities to learn.

Incentive for peer pressure

The final effect of a multi-issue agenda becomes clear if we compare it to another decision-making model – the hub-spoke model. In a hub-spoke model there is an initiator (the father) who tries to convince the other parties (the family members) to agree with his standpoint (a holiday to the US). The initiator does that by negotiating bilaterally with the other parties. The father is the centre of the negotiations – the hub – who maintains relationships with all the other parties – the spokes. Suppose the father doesn't only have the budget for the holiday but is also prepared to reward the family members financially if they vote for the holiday. The first family member manages to negotiate a reward of six units – if the father pays six, this family member will go on the holiday. Then it's the turn of the second family member, who is able to negotiate a reward of seven. A third family member tries to get even more and demands eight as compensation for supporting the holiday.

What is happening here? Because bilateral negotiations are going on, there are strong incentives for the parties to inflate their claims. How is this different to a multi-issue game? If a party inflates its claims in bilateral negotiations, there is only a single party offering a counterbalance. But when a party inflates a claim in a multi-issue game, there are far more opposing powers. As soon as you lay down a high claim, you damage the interests of all the other parties – they will realise that this claim will mean less money for them. In a multi-issue game there are strong incentives for peer pressure – the peers of a party will put pressure on that party if he behaves unreasonably.

Room for the river

The example of the family can be very easily transferred to the real world. Several countries in north-west Europe (Germany, the Netherlands and Belgium) are being confronted with the consequences of global warming. Due to the rising sea level and the melting of glaciers in the Alps, the rivers in these countries must accommodate far more water than previously. As the rivers don't have enough space within their banks to do this, there is a threat of flooding. To prevent flooding, 'retention areas' must be designated: areas that can be allowed to be inundated if rivers threaten to overflow. The regional and local authorities that are designated as retention areas are, naturally, unhappy – the value of their land decreases substantially in order to save other regions from flooding. In other words, one actor pays, another actor profits.

How do you deal with this if several actors have blockade power and can stop the retention areas? As long as it remains a one-issue game – retention area or no retention area – there is a conflict that can degenerate into a stalemate. The decision can also be turned into a multi-issue game. Other issues of concern are the construction of harbours for pleasure boats, floating residential areas, the integration of retention areas into nature reserves, widening canals, improving the road infrastructure and agreements for the construction of business parks. Some of the issues are related to retention areas (floating residential areas), others are not (business parks). That's not the point. What is the point is that an attractive agenda for the involved actors has been created so they will want to participate in the process and the advantages of a multi-issue game can manifest themselves.

The dynamics of multi-issue games

When parties know that decision-making has the character of a multi-issue game, this will bring about extra dynamics.

Parties will anticipate a multi-issue game

Parents who at the beginning of the year receive a request for a pocket-money increase could decide not to respond. They know that sometime in April there will be the annual multi-issue game about the summer holiday, and they will need issues for it. More strategically formulated: If an actor (child) needs another actor (parent) today for an issue (pocket money), it is sensible for this other actor to ask himself whether this issue could be linked to other issues. Tomorrow the roles may be reversed, and the parent needs the support of the child. In which case it would not be sensible to have already agreed to a pocket-money increase.

The example of the family is only a metaphor for real-world decision-making in networks – see the examples of the highway agency in Chapter 2 and room for the river discussed above. In practice emotional ties do play an important role in a family. Let's hope that the strategic game played within a family is not played so intensely as in the outside world of business and government.

The multi-issue game can expand

It is not static. Actors can join in the game – perhaps the oldest daughter's boyfriend will join in at some point and issues can be added to, or removed from, the agenda during the game. Is that a problem? Sometimes it can be. A multi-issue game can become overly complex: So many actors and issues become involved that decision-making becomes impossible. It can become overly simple: too few actors and issues for decisions. Network dynamics can easily frustrate a multi-issues game. In fact, there may be actors who figure this out. They know how a multi-issue game works, and they know how to frustrate such a game – by making it either too complex or too simple. This and other strategies will be discussed in depth in the following chapters. But sometimes the dynamics are absolutely not a problem. The possibilities for arriving at a decision – a *package deal* – can increase. If there's a stalemate, the addition of actors and issues could, in fact, offer space to progress further. Or maybe limiting actors and issues would help because actors blocking the decision-making are no longer involved. It's true that decisions would be made in respect of fewer issues, but a smaller number of decisions are better than no decisions.

Is the desired outcome guaranteed?

This is a burning question in multi-issue games. Suppose the father starts the multi-issue game: Is there a guarantee that in the end the decision will be for the family holiday in the United States? The answer is 'no'. In fact there is a chance that the parties will demand that the father declare the summer holiday negotiable and cancellable at the start of the process. The father obviously does not consider that very attractive, but what's the alternative? As long as it remains a one-issue game, there will be no support for the family holiday. The father has no choice; he has to make it a multi-issue game and declare the summer holiday negotiable.

What can the initiator of a multi-issue game do to have the maximum guarantee that his goal, in this case the family holiday in the US, will have sufficient support?

Think about the design of the multi-issue agenda

Earlier we said that a multi-issue agenda contains gain and pain for every party. For an initiator there is something else to think about. The more issues on the agenda for which other parties are dependent on him, the more possibilities he has of achieving his goal. That would, therefore, be our advice to the father: Try to design the multi-issue game in such a way that the others are sufficiently dependent on you to make it difficult for them to block the holiday. Another strategy could be for the initiator to include several issues the initiator can give way on relatively easily, which will make it more difficult for the others to block the remaining issues.

Play the game intelligently

This will, of course, also influence the ultimate decision-making. The following chapters include an overview of other strategies that can be deployed. It is, for example, important that the discussion about the summer holiday takes place at a good time and that the father still has space to give something away (a shorter holiday, a different programme while there, a layover in Iceland; etc.). These and other strategies offer the initiator a better guarantee of a good outcome than the alternative of a one-issue game.

Have a BATNA option

BATNA (Kim & Fragale, 2005) stands for Best Alternative to a Negotiated Agreement. Suppose that during the multi-issue game the father learns that there really is zero support for the family holiday. The other family members are totally against it, so if the father wants to gain support, he must give the other family members what they want in respect to many other issues, which will be very expensive. The father learns this – one of the advantages of a multi-issue game. He can anticipate this situation by asking himself a simple question: What is my interest here? Think back to the example of the orange in Chapter 2 – behind every standpoint (summer holiday in the US) lies an interest. That could be that the father would like the family to holiday together for at least one more year. If that's the case, he can put one or two other issues on the agenda that serve that interest – for example, a ski trip. The summer holiday might not happen, but one or more BATNAs will give the father the best chances for a good outcome.

Make use of core values and announce the exit option

The previous chapter states that every party has core values that must be protected in every decision-making process. Sometimes an actor can make use of core values. The father would define the summer holiday as a standpoint that affects his core values. He is sombre and thinks he has worked too hard for years and neglected his children. A midlife crisis threatens, and because he wants to revitalise his relationship with his family members, his psychologist has urged him to take a long holiday with his family. (This is, of course, all somewhat exaggerated to make it clear that applying core values to a negotiation is often not easy and can, at times, even be emotionally fraught.) A party in a process can announce that his core values are at stake and that he reserves the right to withdraw from the process if these core values are threatened. It is, on the one hand, a guarantee that the family holiday cannot be blocked by the others. But on the other hand, utilizing the exit option is not always attractive: The other parties can perceive it as intimidation, it puts pressure on the process, and if the exit-option is used, the party concerned still hasn't achieved anything – the father has only blocked a decision against the family holiday.

The power paradox

Whoever cannot achieve his goal in a one-issue game must switch to a multi-issue game – and therefore be prepared to give up their goal. The essence here is that an actor in a network can only achieve his goal by letting go of it. Or put another way, if an actor holds fast to his goal, this actor will definitely not achieve it. This paradox can be traced back to what is called the power paradox (Keltner, 2016). Some actors have many power sources at their command and can, therefore, be tempted to use them to the fullest to achieve their own goals. In a network all the actors – including the actors with many power sources – are dependent on each other. The actor that makes full use of his resources runs the risk of these resources being insufficient for him to achieve his own goals or that he stimulates others to form a coalition of opponents. The actor who shows restraint in the way he uses his power sources, for example as a threat at most, has the greatest chance of influencing others. The paradox is, therefore, that having many power sources only leads to influence over others if these sources are used in a restrained way or not used at all.

Life is no paradise: losers in the multi-issue game

Up to now the assumption has been that the multi-issue game leads to a package deal that is attractive to everyone. Every player gives and takes, and eventually every player is satisfied. This is also called a win-win situation (Simon, Bumpus, & Mann, 2012). A *win-win package deal* – that sounds like paradise; everyone is happy. Of course it doesn't happen like that in the real world, which is why in this section, we will talk about a few misconceptions regarding 'win-win' and analyse the behaviour that could be expected from possible losers.

A positive profit/loss account for every party

The first misconception is that no distinction is made between synergy and win-win situations. Synergy means that, thanks to their cooperation, parties are able to create added value. When a technical university cooperates with a number of technology-intensive companies in its area, synergy can be created. The university benefits, the companies benefit and, in addition, an environment is created that may attract new, technology-intensive companies that will benefit everyone else. The university can, thanks to such an environment, attract more top scientists, and the companies are nearer the source of the knowledge so could be the first to profit from this knowledge.

From a win-win perspective, the question is not so much whether the entirety benefits (synergy) but whether there's a positive profit/loss account for every individual party. Of course, synergy and win-win can come together – however, there are also situations where synergy is possible, without win-win for each player involved.

Suppose that one of the companies, a major player, must incur high costs due to the cooperation. Suppose that this company also sees, with chagrin, that the increase in the number of companies around the university means a proliferation of competition in the region. This company's profit/loss account may be negative. Admittedly there is more cooperation (gain), but this involves additional costs for the company (loss), and the company is also suddenly confronted with increased competition (loss). On balance this company makes a loss. Other companies profit, but this company doesn't, making for a win-lose situation from its perspective. True there is still synergy – the company could even be crucial for the success of the cooperation – but also a win-lose situation, and that could be an incentive for this company to leave the coalition of cooperating parties.

So when it comes to win-win situations, there must always be a positive profit/loss account *per actor*. If it's a synergy situation, it could mean there is also a win-win situation, but this is not, by definition, always the case.

It's all about how the profit is perceived

A second misconception is that 'profit' and 'loss' can always be objectified. If there is talk of a win-win situation *per actor,* the question is always: What does the actor perceive as profit and what as loss? An actor who has made a profit, but not as much as he anticipated, could be very disappointed and, out of frustration, could impede the further progress of the process. It is hardly relevant to brand this behaviour as irrational. It's the perception and recognition of the disappointed actor that is relevant for the progress of the process not an objectification of the profit that suggests he has made enough money.

Perceptions of profit and loss change during the multi-issue game

As mentioned earlier, during the decision-making process actors will learn about its power relationships and content.

These learning processes may bring about a change in their perception of profit and loss. An actor who really wants to achieve issue A could, during the process, learn that the likelihood of achieving this is very small unless he is prepared to accept a lot of compromises. However, during the process issue B arises and has a lot of support. There is a chance that during the process this actor's perception of the profit changes: If B is achieved, this constitutes a profit.

Power plays a major role in influencing perception

In the multi-issue game all the involved parties will try to use their power position to optimise their profit. They will behave strategically and put pressure on the other parties. This exercise of power, which is far from paradisiacal, can have a considerable effect on the perception of the profit. In Chapter 5 this kind of strategy will be discussed in depth.

'Enlarge the shadow of the future'

After the decision regarding the *package* has been made, there is a chance of post-decision opportunism: After banking their own profit, actors start behaving opportunistically. For example, they withdraw from the win-win coalition (Lorenz, 1991, p.186). This is why win-win decision-making has a large temporal component. It's not only important for the actors to be able to establish what each other's prospective profits are, it should also be clear *when* each actor receives their profit. As long as parties still have a prospect of profit, the chance they will behave opportunistically is far lower than it is after they have received it. Paying out the profit too early could be an incentive to behave opportunistically. Axelrod points this out: *Enlarge the shadow of the future* is his advice when it comes to promoting a cooperative attitude (Bó, 2005; Milgrom, 1984, p.126). Dixit and Nalebuff formulate it as follows:

> To avoid the unravelling of trust, there should be no clear final step. As long as there remains a chance of continued business, it will never be

worthwhile to cheat. So when a shady character tells you this will be his last deal before retiring, be especially cautious.

(Dixit & Nalebuff, 1991, p.158)

Management of losers

To reiterate, win-win decision-making does not alter the fact that decision-making can result in losers. These are the parties who have no share in the package deal. Either they have not participated in the process, although the decision might adversely affect their interests, or they have withdrawn from the process during the compilation of the package deal because there were not enough prospects of profit for them. Back to the family (really for the last time): The boyfriend of the elder daughter did not participate in the decision-making and is very unhappy that his girlfriend will be spending three weeks in the United States without him. In such a situation we can say that for the family members this is a win-win situation, but for other parties (the boyfriend) it's a *win-lose* situation. These losers can gain from fighting against the *win-win package*. This means the coalition will have to invest in 'loser management'– particularly when the losers have a power position from which to fight against the package deal or when these parties will still be needed in the future. The parties in the coalition must, for example, be flexible enough to also allow losers to join when they become too much of a threat to the coalition. This flexibility also relates to the content of the package deal: The participation of new parties can change the content of the package.

Losers: behaviour patterns

How do losers behave? What are their type of behaviour patterns, and what are the strategies to get on well with them again?

Losers form coalitions with other parties

A loser can go in search of allies. These are parties who have also been adversely affected by the decision and have an interest in either reversing it or impeding its implementation.

Losers exploit meetings elsewhere

A loser can make strategic use of the fact that in the future, and related to other issues, he will meet the partners in the win-win coalition once again. Perhaps when they meet again the parties who made the win-win decision will really need the support of the loser. The loser's strategy could be that he feeds this 'the loser will be needed in the future' perception. For the parties in the win-win coalition, this can mean that the profit/loss account of the package changes. If there are no active losers in the game, the calculation is:

- [Revenues of the package] – [Costs of the package]

If there are active losers in the game, the calculation is different:

- [Revenues of the package] – [Costs of the package] – [Costs of future processes in which the losers are involved]

This can mean that these parties are no longer in profit, which means their support of the coalition partners and the package no longer goes without saying.

Losers try to uncouple parties from the win-win coalition

When a win-win coalition has been formed, it can include a number of parties who are not loyal or hardly loyal. Perhaps these parties' profit/loss accounts are only narrowly positive or they have already received their profit. It is also possible that, due to changing circumstances, some parties in the coalition see their profit/loss account worsening. These are potential allies for the losers.

Losers can create a small risk of a major disaster

When the actors in the coalition run a small risk of a major disaster, this can be a strong incentive for them to withdraw from the coalition. Not only the loss but also the costs of the risk created by the loser will be deducted from any future profit they will receive.

For example: A party who has been shut out of the package deal can instigate legal proceedings against the package. Even if the chance of success is small, this means that for a long time (proceedings can take a long time) a sword of Damocles will hang over the heads of the 'winners'. There is a chance, however small, that the agreements related to the package are not legally tenable. This can strengthen the loser's position.

Losers challenge the legitimacy of the decision on the grounds of exclusion

Another strategy is that a loser invokes the fact that he was not involved in the decision-making process. This single fact can threaten the win-win situation when several parties in a coalition have doubts about the package. They then have a procedure-related reason to leave the coalition. They can argue that the single fact that certain parties were excluded is sufficient reason to terminate their support of the win-win coalition. Parties can invoke procedural arguments without the need for any discussion related to the package content.

Losers opt for catch as catch can

The loser can sometimes be 'wounded' in the heart of his interests. When this is the case, the result can be that the loser uses a *catch as catch can* strategy to fight the coalition. The package is fought against using any available means and without any respect for accepted codes of conduct. This can be an unfair fight because the winners are expected to comply with accepted codes of conduct.

Counterstrategies

So, win-win package deals face two risks. Risk 1 is that actors who have already enjoyed their profit (or for whom the profit/loss balance is no longer positive for other reasons) will leave the coalition. Risk two is that actors who for one reason or another are dissatisfied with the outcome will try to derail the win-win package.

These are several strategies to deal with this. The core characteristic of these strategies is to prevent, as far as possible, a hard confrontation between winners and losers.

Ensure a continuous win-win process

The involved actors must always be able to look forward to profit. This can be the reason to generate new possibilities for profit. Thanks to the win-win coalition, the involved parties maintain intense relationships. They are, naturally, confronted with new problems and solutions and can link these to the problems and solutions of their fellow coalition members. As a result new possibilities for win-win situations will arise, which may offer opportunities to involve the initial losers. The creation of a win-win situation is, therefore, not a one-off activity but a continuous process.

Keep relationships with losers open

It may be necessary to invite one of more of the losers to join the coalition during the process, for example because the blockade power of the loser(s) has become too great.

This will change the content of the package deal. This may be disappointing for the original coalition members, but it will make the deal more achievable. Certain actions can be such a threat for the win-win coalition that it is necessary to invite the loser to join the coalition.

Compensate losers elsewhere

Losers can be compensated elsewhere in relation to other issues. Parties with redundant relationships will also meet the loser during other processes involving other issues and can use these relationships to compensate the loser (Monnikhof, 2006, p.125).[1]

Give winners enough prospects of profit

Continuously making it clear to coalition members that they have a positive profit/loss account is also important. When the members are convinced of this, the chance that the strategies of losers will succeed is far smaller than in a situation in which the winners have doubts regarding their profit/loss account. What is important here is that the members of the win-win coalition are aware that opportunistic behaviour or withdrawal from the coalition could disrupt the relationship with fellow coalition members and thus make future cooperation related to other issues more difficult.

Frame the loss as a loss for all parties

When a loss is actually inflicted on a number of parties, it is important that the loss is defined, as far as possible, as a collective loss ('everyone is a loser', 'there is no winner') or that the loser is told that his loss has entitled him to future compensation or profit. Both strategies can moderate the loser's behaviour.

This chapter began with the statement that it would be about the content. In multi-issue processes the focus is, to a great extent, on the content. It will, however, be clear that this can never be viewed in isolation from the power relationships in a network. A multi-issue game is the reflection of the power relationships in a network. And the outcome of the content of a multi-issue game falls prey to a power-play between winners and losers.

A distinction between content and power, or between content and game, may exist in theory, but in real life this is not the case.

Note

1 What's more, the less actors are involved in decision-making, the less likely they are to agree with a proposal for compensation.

4 A process, not a project

Why project management does not work

Where are we now? Decision-making in a network is a complex business: There are many players, unstructured problems and shifting dynamics. This demands that the actors in a network develop strategies to come to decision-making. Actors will analyse the other actors and use their relationship network. But to achieve collective decision-making you need more – making a collective decision must be made attractive for the actors involved. That requires process management and an agenda that is, in terms of content, sufficiently appealing for the actors to participate in the collective decision-making. In other words, you need a multi-issue agenda.

All these strategies also teach us that in a network decision-making is a process of interaction between the parties – and not a project that progresses in a linear fashion steered by a project manager, which is the case in a hierarchy. In this chapter we're going to talk about a number of supplementary strategies. These strategies build on the previous two chapters and will be identified through a systematic comparison between decision-making as a project (which assumes a hierarchy) and decision-making as a process (which is what happens in a network).

Project versus process

Decision-making in a project has three key characteristics.

First, decision-making progresses in a number of logical phases that follow each other in sequence. For example:

- Problem formulation;
- Goal determination;
- Information gathering;
- Decision-making;
- Implementation; and
- Evaluation

Second, a project approach sets great store by precision, sharpness, unequivocality and focus. A problem must be described as precisely and lucidly as possible, and goals must be clear-cut, because that's how to create focus and direction in the decision-making process.

Third, planning is very important. It must be clear, in advance, which phases will be achieved when and what the deadlines and decision gates are – the more precise the planning and the better this is prepared up front, the more predictable the decision-making.

Because a project assumes that either there will be one person who takes the lead or that the involved actors are in agreement regarding the project, in a network none of this will work. In the following paragraphs we will go through the phases of a project-based approach and in each case indicate what the alternative strategies are if the decision-making is a process not a project.

Problem formulation: precise problem definitions are not attractive

In a project-based approach to decision-making, the first observation will be that there is a problem. A content analysis will enable the problem to be demarcated, which is important: A clear-cut demarcation of a problem helps when finding a solution.

The next question is *when* must a problem be formulated? In a project-based approach a problem goes before the solution – first there's the problem, then the solution. And if a problem arises, it must be solved. Solve a problem too late and the damage could be enormous. What are the main differences between that and a process-based approach?

Influence the problem perception – so formulate problems in broad terms

In networks it's a very different story. An actor who defines a problem must be aware that THE problem doesn't exist. There is 'only' problem perception, and the question is whether other actors have the same perception of the problem (Guba & Lincoln, 1989).

Table 4.1 Problems in a project and in a process

Project-based decision-making	*Process-based decision-making*
There is a problem, so a content analysis is required.	There is a perception of a problem, so the perceptions of others should be influenced.
The problem is clearly demarcated.	The problem is formulated in broad terms.
The problem steers the solution.	The solution steers the problem.
A problem is solved when it arises.	The moment at which a problem is formulated is a strategic choice. The *window of opportunity* must be open.

If the problem is more or less objectified, as in project-based decision-making, analysis of the content of this problem is the key to solving this problem. When problem perceptions take centre stage, an actor has to influence the problem perception of other actors.

A problem demarcation that is too clear-cut can be dysfunctional in a process. Indeed, the more clear-cut the problem demarcation, the greater the chance that the other parties, with their varying opinions and interests, will not support the problem definition. In many cases it is more sensible to formulate a problem in broad terms. The broader the formulation, the greater the chance it includes components that are attractive for many actors.

To illustrate this, think of a port authority that wants to construct an offshore port due to a shortfall of capacity in the existing port area. If the problem formulation is clear-cut (there is a capacity shortfall of four thousand hectares, which means the port cannot expand), there is a chance that certain parties will be against the project because they don't recognise the problem. Opponents could come from the business community (who may see the expansion as a threat to their economic power position or are anxious about increasing congestion on the roads around the port), municipalities (adverse effect on tourism), environmental organisations (damage to a nature reserve) or other ports (competition). When these parties ask themselves 'What's in it for me?' the answer is: nothing.

However, formulate a problem in broad terms– for example, the region's ecological and economic infrastructures are weak, how can they be strengthened? – then, in principle, every party has a chance to achieve its own goals. By formulating the problem in broad terms, the other parties may also be able to achieve their goals, rather than just the port authority. For these other parties there is at least a chance of a positive answer to the question 'What's in it for me?'

Connect solutions to problems

Another major difference between the two approaches is the sequence of problem formulation and solution. In a project-based approach the logical sequence is first a problem is defined and then a solution is sought. In a network the sequence can be the other way around. 'Solutions looking for problems' is how Aaron Wildavsky once described this phenomenon. Suppose the port authority needs the minister of infrastructure's support for the port expansion. The port authority would really like to construct an offshore port, but the minister has totally different priorities. Global warming is raising the sea level, and the problem of safety and coastline reinforcement is on the minister's agenda. Money must be made available for this, so there's less available for the port.

Anyone who knows the problem of the other actor, in this case the minister, and who needs this other actor can try to link his own solution to the other actor's problem. The port authority could propose an offshore port configured in such a way that it contributes towards coastline reinforcement, for example by having a favourable effect on currents so they become less of a threat to safety. The consequence of this is that the offshore port has suddenly become a solution to the minister's problem, which means there's a greater chance that the minister will support this new port.

So, problems are linked to solutions if this increases other parties' support for this solution. Unlinking is also possible if a linkage stands in the way of problem-solving. The picture this creates of a decision-making process is one of a continuous linking and unlinking of problems and solutions.

Watch for the window of opportunity

Finally, the *moment* at which a problem is formulated is a strategic choice. In a project-based approach a problem is pointed out when it appears. In a process-based approach far more attention is paid to the *window of opportunity*, the moment at which the chance of support for the problem formulation is sufficient (Kingdon, 1984). The concept is derived from the *launch window* in space travel. A launch window (Li, Li, & Jiang, 2008) is a particular moment in time – sometimes only minutes, sometimes several days – during which the launch or return of a space craft is possible.

All kinds of situation can be imagined in which problem A has either a small or large chance of a solution – in which the window of opportunity is shut or open.

- There are too many competing problems, which means too little attention for problem A. Actors wait until there is more space on the agenda, so the window of opportunity is shut.
- The inverse is also a possibility: Because there are so many competing problems, very little attention is being paid to problem A. As a result there is also very little opposition to the proposed solution. The window of opportunity is open.
- If the *sense of urgency* of the other parties in the network is limited, the window of opportunity is shut. The first task is to instil a sense of urgency in the other parties through the strategy of priming.
- The problem isn't 'sexy'; it doesn't, for example, reflect the spirit of the times or the current strategic agenda. Pleas for privacy protection have less chance of support in a period in which there is anxiety regarding terrorist attacks than in calmer times. By contrast, someone who puts problems related to security on the agenda has a good chance that the window of opportunity is open.

Goals: clear goals get in your way

In a project-based approach a goal is THE reference point in a decision-making process. If during the process parties are unsure about what actions they should take, they can always refer to the goal: How will the action concerned contribute towards achieving the goal? Clearly formulated goals give direction to the decision-making.

In a project-based approach, goals are, of course, set at the beginning of the decision-making process. Without goals the decision-making process will have no direction and course. Clearly formulated goals encourage a good progress of this process. Goals are derived from the problem formulation.

Broad and vague goals

In a network of many parties with differing interests, clearly formulated goals are far less sensible (Ordóñez, Schweitzer, Galinsky, & Bazerman, 2009).

First and foremost, a party that formulates a goal clearly in advance, and tells other parties about it, jeopardises its position in the game. Specifying your goals in advance makes you a less pliable party who cannot react as flexibly to new and unforeseen developments as, for example, in the multi-issue game.

In addition, a party's goals – what a party wants to achieve – are sometimes strategic information. If party A has a goal and party B knows what it is, party B also knows exactly what party A must do to achieve that goal. So, formulating clear goals in advance may be very unwise.

There are also content-related reasons for not formulating goals in advance. A characteristic of the decision-making process in a network is that it progresses very erratically. Many actors are involved, and there are many issues on the agenda. This agenda can, certainly in the beginning, keep changing. This means new opportunities for parties can keep appearing. Seizing these opportunities is perhaps more important than achieving goals formulated in advance. Going back to the offshore port example: Perhaps the port authority's original goal was to achieve a four thousand-hectare offshore port for container transshipment. Then begins the game with other actors, some of whom – for example the environmental movement, the local seaside resorts and the minister of infrastructure who is responsible for coastline protection – are against the project. During the process new issues keep popping up. Perhaps the offshore port can also contribute towards a better recreational infrastructure (interest of seaside resorts), protecting against a rising sea level

Table 4.2 Goals in a project and in a process

Project-based decision-making	Process-based decision-making
Unambiguous and clearly formulated goals that give direction to the decision-making.	Broad or even vague goals. Clear-cut goals obstruct learning and are strategically unadvisable.
Goals are formulated in advance.	Goals arise during a process.
Well-defined scope	*Flexible scope*

(interest of the minister) and/or the creation of new nature reserves (interest of environmental movement). These are all opportunities that can contribute not only towards gaining more support from the important players but also towards a different and better plan content. These opportunities mean that the port authority's goals keep shifting – from four thousand hectares for container transshipment to additional hectares for recreation, nature and security. It can go further: Perhaps the port authority is prepared to give up the offshore port if space is made to expand the existing inland port. Being alert to opportunities that arise is more important than formulating goals as precisely as possible in advance – goals arise during a process. 'Goal-seeking behaviour' during the process is often more effective than working with fixed goals at the start of the process. Goal-seeking refers to the countless opportunities that come along during a decision-making process, so every actor should constantly be on the lookout for the goals he can achieve.

The scope of the process is constantly moving

The goal-seeking character of the decision-making process also has consequences for the scope of a process. In a project-based approach, a project has a fixed scope, which must be monitored, and 'scope creep' must be avoided if at all possible.

In a network specifying a scope is problematic. It implies that there is a party that can impose its scope on other parties. Perhaps at least as important, an *ex ante* formulated and fixed scope can restrict the *decision-making space* and, as a result of that, can hamper the goal-seeking behaviour and learning processes of the involved actors – and thus reduce the possibilities for package deals. When an initiator has a problem and formulates a fixed scope, this initiator is not a very attractive partner for the others because they cannot see enough possibilities for solving their own problems.

A nice detail to finish with: It's understandable that a maritime people like the Dutch should have many sayings based on shipping. Many of these sayings are good metaphors for the project-based approach. For example, 'A ship has only one captain', who 'steers a clear course' and preferentially also goes 'full steam ahead'. A 'zigzag course' is out of the question. And if anyone dares to criticise, he or she is very quickly reminded that '*de beste stuurlui aan wal staan*', which translates literally as 'the best helmsmen stand on the shore'. In other words, the watchers always think they know better than the doers.

In a network these metaphors really do not work. On a network 'ship' there are by definition a number of captains who are dependent on each other. When one of the captains opts for a 'clear course', it's very likely this will only lead to opposition and resistance from the other captains, who have other opinions regarding the course that should be steered. Going 'full steam ahead' is also not very sensible: It's an incentive for opposition and limits the possibilities for content-related learning and the adjustment of goals. A zigzag course can be an intelligent way of 'going with the flow'. And even if the best helmsmen are on the shore, if an actor needs them, he must consult with them, however irritating these 'helmsmen' may be.

Wanting to be 'in the lead' also fits in with such metaphors; in a network this can be dysfunctional. An actor who is active in a network is always looking for new links between problems and solutions. Making such links is a continuous process. This means that an actor will be active in many processes and being 'in the lead' in all of them is impossible. It might be more effective to sit 'in the slipstream' waiting for a window of opportunity that links a problem and a solution. Think of a cyclist who is in the lead for most of the race. Nine times out of ten he will not be the first to cross the finish line. The cyclist who rode in his slipstream for most of the race will bide his time because there will always be a gap (a window) in which he can sprint past and be first across the line.

Information: the right information doesn't exist

In a project-based decision-making process information is a crucial power source. Good decision-making is impossible without timely and good information. What information an actor needs is determined by the nature of the problem definition and the chosen goal. This information will be accumulated on a *need to know* basis: Only the information that is needed to solve the problem is relevant for an actor. The general opinion is also that, to a great extent, the quality of the decision-making depends on the quality of the information.

In a process-based approach information gathering and provision are very actor-bound, which has several major consequences.

The necessity of negotiated knowledge

Earlier in this book we described what 'unstructured' problems are. The essence of this type of problem is that they cannot be objectified. The information that underpins the problem analysis is always debatable or prone to

Table 4.3 Information in a project and in a process

Project-based decision-making	*Process-based decision-making*
Objectify information as far as possible	Create negotiated knowledge
Clear-cut distinction between information gathering and decision-making	Information gathering and decision-making run into each other
The right information leads to the right decision	The right process leads to the right decision
The leading principle for gathering information: need to know	The leading principle for information gathering: nice to know

differences (due to the data, methods and system boundaries used). In addition, problem analysis always demands nominative choices, which are also debatable. The information that underpins actor A's problem analysis or decision doesn't necessarily have to be authoritative in actor B's opinion. There are no objective analyses or solutions for unstructured problems.

Nowadays unstructured problems are everywhere, but in a network they have an extra dimension. The parties in a network have different interests and, therefore, strong incentives to debate the information and problem analyses of other parties. This implies that in a network situation the unstructured character of a problem is often magnified.

This creates a troublesome dilemma. On the one hand, information is necessary if a good decision is to be reached; on the other hand, the information is often neither objective nor incontestable. The way out of this dilemma is that the parties negotiate the correctness of the information. When every party has an individual view of a problem and has relevant expertise, the parties must, together, establish what is good information. We call the result of this process *negotiated knowledge*. Negotiation about information is, therefore, not a sign of unjustified relativity (i.e., everything is negotiable, even facts) but the only way to deal responsibly with the disputable nature of information challenges when formulating policy (Lidskog & Sundqvist, 2004).

Suppose that the safety of an airport must be determined. This is impossible to objectify. Only a limited amount of data is available: The number of accidents at modern airports is too limited to build up reliable data banks. System boundaries are disputable: Must the analysis include only the airport itself or also a ring around the airport? If a ring is included, how wide should it be – one kilometre, ten kilometres, forty kilometres? What method must be used to determine the safety? How should technological and social changes be handled? Suppose, for example, that new technology makes aircraft even safer, how should that fact influence safety analyses? Such questions could be asked when, for example, the noise nuisance or the environmental impact of an airport must be calculated. It will be clear that different parties on and around the airport have very different opinions regarding the choices that must be made in respect of these points (Petts, 2003; Weible, Sabatier, & Lubell, 2004).

The striving for negotiated knowledge means that parties must come to an understanding regarding the questions of which data, system boundaries and methods will be used and how technological and social dynamism will be handled (Andrews & Delahaye, 2000). Such understanding can, of course, only take place if the parties have sufficient incentive to arrive at negotiated knowledge. The most important incentive is often the unattractiveness of the alternative. If the parties do not strive for negotiated knowledge, it can lead to a *free for all fight*. Every party has its own calculations and models, and the parties don't agree on anything. The resulting chaos is unattractive to many parties. In the example of the airport, this means that its position is continuously open to discussion, and those opposed will have the idea that the airport can do what it likes because there is no consensus regarding the safety level.

Naturally experts also play a role in the creation of negotiated knowledge. They will supply their analyses, and they will be a component of the negotiated knowledge acquisition process. They are not, therefore, the experts who one-sidedly announce what the facts are but rather experts who go through the process of creating negotiated knowledge with each other and with the stakeholders. Experts can influence that process. They can make it clear to the stakeholders that some opinions really are nonsense from a scientific perspective. They can inject the latest scientific insights into the process – the experts often have information the stakeholders do not have. On the other hand, the stakeholders will also challenge the experts to specify which knowledge is 'hard' and which is 'soft', which information is debatable, and which methods are being used and whether there are alternative methods.

Information gathering and decision-making merge together

In a project-based approach information gathering and decision-making are two separate and sequential phases: The decision-making doesn't take place until the information gathering has been completed. When creating negotiated knowledge, the two phases merge together. Suppose there is discussion regarding the airport's safety and that different parties have different opinions regarding the data to be used and the system boundaries to be adhered to.

How can the parties arrive at negotiated knowledge?

- When parties disagree about the data to be used or the system boundaries, sensitivity analyses can be carried out to determine how sensitive the outcomes of an analysis will be using different data sets. It may be that the outcomes have only a limited sensitivity, in which case the dispute over the data to be used and the system boundaries is no longer relevant.
- Perhaps it transpires that different data sets lead to very different outcomes. According to one data set, the airport is safe; according to another, it is not. If that is the case, a discussion about which data set to use will never lead to a consensus. The discussion may then shift. If there's a difference in safety, there are measures that could be taken through which the danger that according to some data is present will be reduced.

This shifts the attention away from achieving a consensus regarding the right data set and towards the question of whether decisions can be made through which it no longer matters that the outcomes of the analyses are different. As a result the information phase and the decision-making phase merge together. Disagreement regarding information is solved by making decisions whereby the disagreement is no longer relevant.

One major risk is that during the negotiation process parties arrive at a form of negotiated knowledge that conflicts with the current state of knowledge. Negotiated knowledge can degenerate into negotiated nonsense. However, this risk, too, cannot lead to the conclusion that negotiated knowledge should be discounted. On the contrary, this risk can be prevented by also involving parties in the negotiation process who know the current state of knowledge in a particular field. These parties will often be content experts who, as we said, will not play the classic role in this instance (the supply of the 'objective' information). Their input will be their insights: They will confront the other parties with the current state of knowledge and will, in their turn, also be questioned by the other parties regarding the robustness of this knowledge. In this way they facilitate the negotiation process (Ravetz, 1999).

The right process leads to the right decision

In a project the right information leads to the right decision. In a process the right information doesn't exist. In most cases the key factor is a good process: Are the most important actors invited; do they have a reasonable and fair opportunity to influence the agenda; can they influence the decision-making; are their core values protected? A good process is, therefore, conducive to the support of the involved actors and the eventual result. As previously stated, the involvement of experts, which results in high-quality negotiated knowledge, can also be a component of a good process.

Nice-to-know information gathering

In a network decision-making proceeds erratically and appears chaotic. How does the information gathering process take place in such a process? What are the fundamental principles?

In project-based thinking the *need to know* principle (Vuori, 2006) is dominant. There is a clear goal, and only information that is useful for the achievement of this goal is relevant. All other information leads only to information overload.

In a network *nice to know* is more effective. Nice-to-know information gathering doesn't have a clear focus. Actors try, via their relationships, to glean as much information as possible out of the network, even when it is not immediately clear what purpose this information will serve. The decision-making will progress erratically, so there will always be unexpected opportunities or obstacles. The more information actors have, the better they can deal with this unpredictability. They know the problems of the other actors, which makes it easier to link their own problems to the problems of the others. They know, for example, which issues affect other parties and thanks to this can draw up a multi-issue agenda that these parties find attractive.

Decision-making is only ticking off what has already been decided

In the project-based approach a decision is an important moment. The problem and goal have been formulated, information has been gathered and so a decision can be made. The decision-making will have a considerable influence on the further progress of the project, it is a *go* or a *no go* moment – a decision is made to turn left or turn right.

In a process-based approach a decision is far more nuanced.

In a network decision-making is the result of a process in which parties have negotiated about many issues. The formal agreement of the package will generally no longer be a surprise for these parties. They have raised their issues, gone through the consultation and negotiation processes and drawn up a package. The formal decision-making is a question of 'ticking the boxes' – the already negotiated decision must be recorded formally. The formal decision-making will, therefore, be far less of a guide for the direction to be taken than it is in a project-based approach. The direction has already been determined during the process that preceded the formal decision-making. This is not to say that the relationship between the process and the formal decision-making always runs smoothly or will never involve tensions. We will come back to this in Chapter 5.

Decision-making is an ongoing process with new rounds and new opportunities

There's something else. A formal decision almost never means the end of a decision-making process. In Chapter 3 we said that in the negotiations related to issues A – D, the losers in respect to issue A can be compensated in the decision-making in respect to issue B, C or D. Although the decision-making related to A appears to be settled, it does in fact influence the decision-making related to issues B to D. Parties can make proactive use of this mechanism: They accept a loss in respect to issue A on condition that they are compensated during the decision-making related to issue B. This makes

Table 4.4 Decision making in a project and in a process

Project-based decision-making	*Process-based decision-making*
The decision follows on from problem, goal, information	After the decision there is a following round, so new opportunities exist
Making the decision explicit gives direction	Making the decision explicit makes it vulnerable – it generates incentives for resistance
Phased planning	Tempo changes
Project management techniques (tight planning, deadlines)	Project management techniques are dysfunctional
Project-based activity and communication	Process-based activity and project-based communication

decision-making an *ongoing process*. The decision-making related to B cannot be understood without an insight into the decision-making related to A, and the decision-making related to A was probably influenced by earlier decision-making processes.

Open-ended decision-making

In a hierarchy a decision that can be completely 'cut and dried' is attractive. A detailed decision that offers little room to manoeuvre is an important guarantee that the implementation will conform to the decision. In a network a decision is usually a package deal. In principle such a deal has a win-win character: Each party wins more than it loses. This win-win character is the guarantee that the implementation will conform to the decision because it is in the interest of every party.

Decision-making can also be a win-lose game: Certain parties don't win. In a win-lose game a cut-and-dried decision deprives the losing parties of any perspective of profit and can be an incentive for them to adopt catch-as-catch-can behaviour. Every opportunity to frustrate the implementation will be seized. We call it an open-ended decision-making when certain options are kept open, which means there are still opportunities in the future for every party. In a network open-ended decision-making has a positive connotation: It's an incentive for cooperative behaviour.

An example: At a certain moment a decision to extend a harbour by constructing an offshore port is made in a network. This decision can have winners and losers. The losers may have an incentive to frustrate the decision – there's nothing more to be won. That will certainly be the case if the decision is completely cut and dried. But it's different if the decision is open-ended – if, for example, it is decided that an offshore port will be constructed, but the question of which activities will be carried out in the offshore port has remained open. That could mean new prospects of profit for the losers. An environmental organisation that was against the offshore port is a loser but still has a chance of being a winner if, for example, a portion of the harbour expansion area is designated as woodland.

There are content-related, as well as strategic, arguments for open-ended decision-making. The idea that an all-encompassing decision related to a complex issue can be made in one fell swoop is based on the assumption that all the relevant information is available to the decision-maker(s) at that moment. This is an unrealistic assumption. Virtually nobody has such omnipotence. Herbert Simon called it the *bounded rationality* of decision-makers (Simon, 1961). Bounded rationality makes integral, overall decisions impossible (Williamson, 1989). A decision will, therefore, always be partial and incomplete. This makes additions to the decision in the course of time unavoidable. Actors will be aware of this: There are still opportunities for them, which could be a reason for continuing to have a cooperative attitude. On top of that, these open spaces in decisions also mean possibilities to learn and make additions or amendments to the initial decision so that in the end it is better.

Planning and deadlines are dysfunctional

Project-based decision-making is often characterised by a crucial role for plans – which aspects of the decision-making must be finalised and planned for in advance. In a project plans and deadlines are useful for good decision-making. A deadline gives the involved parties an incentive to make progress and to ensure the deadline is met.

In a network plans and deadlines can weaken an actor's negotiating position. If there are many actors with different interests and one of the actors wants to achieve a project before a specified deadline without fail, this will have absolutely no effect on the other actors. They don't want that, and without their support the project will come to nothing. More to the point, a deadline often hinders the actor who sets it. An actor sets a deadline, but it means nothing to those opposed to it. Who has the problem if the deadline isn't met? The actor concerned – not his opponents. When is the best time for the opponents to negotiate with this actor? Just before the deadline – that's when there's the best chance the actor will give a lot away in order to achieve the deadline. Setting a deadline can weaken an actor's position in a network because it's an incentive for delay.

Tempo changes

Process-based decision-making is generally characterised by tempo changes. A delay in decision-making can sometimes be sensible, for example, while waiting for sufficient attention or a window of opportunity – a sudden opportunity for a link to a new problem or solution (Kingdon, 1984). When such a window opens, actors can suddenly accelerate and achieve many links.

Backstage and frontstage: process-based activity, project-based communication

When a decision has been made, some form of external communication is always required. A company that makes a major investment decision must communicate this to its own employees, the shareholders and probably the media as well. The same applies for political players – they must communicate with a parliament, constituents and the media. Even the family negotiating about a holiday in Chapter 3 will communicate their decision to the neighbours, friends and relatives.

Communication means the degree of logic in the decision must be explained. In a network there is always a negotiating logic hiding behind a decision: The parties have undergone a process of interaction, with a multi-issue-agenda, have made links between problems and solutions and, ultimately, have put a package deal together. The problem now is that the communicative power of this negotiating logic is limited. What happens when a decision is communicated to the 'neighbours' – the parties that did not participate in the process – with an explanation of how the negotiations went? For example, the government announces that it has decided to construct an offshore port as part of a package that also included more supple immigration regulations, a new nature reserve and more money for education. The accusations are obvious:

- *Content-related accusations*: The decision is opportunistic. It was not based on a thorough analysis of problems and solutions or on clear choices. It was the result of negotiations. If other parties had been sitting round the table or if certain parties had behaved more intelligently or if other issues had been on the agenda, the outcome would have been different.
- *Procedural accusations*: The way the decision was arrived at was not visible. Some of the parties played a strategic game out of the public's sight. That conflicts with the values that virtually every private and public organisation sets great store by – a commitment to 'transparency' and 'open government' and an aversion to 'game playing' and 'back rooms'.

By contrast, in terms of communication, a project-based approach is very powerful. Anyone who defends a decision in project management language – thorough problem analyses, clear goals, good information – is unlikely to be accused of opportunism. The decision was based on thorough analysis and a number of clear starting points (versus opportunism). The creation of the decision took place totally transparently: phases were formulated in advance, worked through one at a time, maybe in accordance with a predetermined schedule (versus invisibility).

This sketch creates a problematic dilemma. The previous chapters (hopefully) made it clear that a project-based approach has little chance of success in a network of interdependencies. However, in terms of communication, the project-based approach is very powerful. The reverse applies for a process-based approach: suitable for networks but limited in communication power. So, the question is: How do you solve this dilemma?

The simplest answer to this question is to utilise the strengths of both approaches: The *activity* in a network is process-based; the *communication* of the results of the process takes place in project-based language. In this context David A. Buchanan and David Boddy make a distinction between *frontstage activities* and *backstage activities* (Buchanan & Boddy, 1992, p.27, 133). The backstage activities are shaped by the power game. Parties devise a multi-issue game, broaden the agenda, link and unlink issues, try to put together a package deal, etc. The outcomes of this process are presented in the *public performance,* or on the frontstage, where the dominant language is that of project management. Young referred to the importance of this. Like *policy effectiveness, policy expressiveness* is an important value. Can policy be expressive? Does it appeal to the values and feelings of other actors? The language of the hierarchy – decisiveness, clarity, daring – is, as far as this policy expressiveness is concerned, often more powerful than the language of the network – consultation, negotiation, interaction.

Suppose that a number of parties in a company are negotiating in a multi-issue game involving three issues: a possible investment in new equipment, a change to the planning and control cycle, and an amendment to the marketing strategy. Eventually they reach agreement and make a package-deal decision. One component of this decision is that the planning and control cycle will become more flexible: The business units will have to produce fewer figures, and auditing by the central staff departments will be less stringent. This fulfils a long-cherished wish of the business units.

This decision must be communicated. This decision could be legitimised with an appeal to the negotiating logic: The planning and control cycle will be more flexible and, in exchange for this, the business units will be subjected to more central control in respect of marketing. The communicative power of this is limited: The idea that this is a case of horse-trading could take root. However, the decision could also be communicated in project-based language:

- There was a problem: Over the years the planning and control cycle had become so overly detailed and unwieldy that it had led to too great a bureaucratic burden;
- There was a goal: debureaucratisation and revitalisation of the planning and control cycle;
- Information was gathered: which aspects of the planning and control cycle were overly bureaucratic and thus dysfunctional and which were functional;
- A decision was made;
- This will be implemented and evaluated.

Such a strategy – process-based activity backstage, project-based communication frontstage – combines the best of two worlds.

Is this, in fact, pure opportunism? Horse-trading in the back room packaged as rational decision-making? It can be, naturally, but it isn't always. The fact that *during* a process the parties know that *after* the process they must communicate the result in project-based language can also create *disincentives* for opportunism and horse-trading. At the end of the process, they must explain the result in content-related terms. If the legitimacy of the package deal is based solely on horse-trading, legitimising the decision is problematic. Parties can use this fact during the process to encourage other parties to behave reasonably and desist from horse-trading. They can point out to the other parties in the network that they cannot explain certain results of the process because they look too much like the results of horse-trading. In other words, the need for legitimisation and communication in project-based language at the end of the process generates incentives for moderate behaviour during the process.

Intermezzo: the risks of plan-do-check-act thinking

Parties carry out all kinds of activities and then, eventually, the result of these activities is recorded in a formal decision, a policy document or a plan. This observation is far from original, but it's still difficult to underestimate its importance. Many people have the idea in their head that the result is first recorded and then implemented. This picture translates into all kinds of approaches to change, for example the well-known *plan-do-check-act cycle* (PDCA) (Moen & Norman, 2006). The PDCA cycle is accredited to W. Edwards Deming and is, in essence, a simple way to initiate changes. A problem analysis is carried out and solutions formulated that are laid-down in a blueprint (plan). The plan is implemented (do). After a time the success of the plan is evaluated: Have the intended results been achieved (check)? If not this can lead to the plan being amended or adjusted. If the implementation is in order, the new way of working becomes part of the daily routine in an organisation (Act). The circle can then be gone round again but at a higher level of complexity and related to more complicated problems. Anyone who uses this cycle as a reference framework for looking at change processes runs a number of risks:

- The PDCA cycle obstructs the view of the reality behind the formal policy, plan or decision. These documents cannot be understood without an insight into the underlying process.
- The PDCA cycle obstructs the view of the reality surrounding the formal decision-making process. Not all the results of the interaction process will be laid down in formal documents. Some things just happen: Parties make and fulfil agreements without them being drawn up in a formal document.
- The PDCA cycle leads to wrong judgments. PDCA thinking means a policy, plan or decision is required before action can be taken. If parties in a process achieve results but this is not written down in a plan, accusations of opportunism soon may be forthcoming. In PDCA thinking omitting to record something in a plan, for example a policy, is wrong, although very good results can be achieved without a policy.
- The PDCA cycle leads to bureaucratisation. When the accusation of opportunism is widespread, it can be a reason for parties to invest more in the drawing up of formal plans or policy documents. The question is: What is the added value of this when it is totally unnecessary?
- The PDCA cycle leads to inertia. Parties state their goals and milestones in their formal documentation and, as a result, have less space for consultation and negotiation in the process. PDCA thinking has then become a barrier and can lower the quality of the decision-making process.

Does this mean that every form of PDCA thinking is fundamentally wrong? Of course not. PDCA is more appropriate in a context in which there is a form of hierarchy, a structured problem and a measure of stability. In a situation involving a network, unstructured problems and dynamics, PDCA can play a role when parties have agreed a package deal and now want to implement the package.

Why is PDCA-based thinking so popular despite the drawbacks? There are at least two reasons:

- The first is that the schematics of PDCA thinking offer certainty. Anyone confronted with a network's erratic decision-making who doesn't see the underlying mechanisms – actors, interests and strategies – can be overwhelmed by the apparent chaos in which he or she has landed. PDCA-based thinking schematics offer clarity and promise: They imply that decision-making can also proceed in an orderly, structured way. It will be clear from the above summary about the risks of PDCA thinking that this promise will not be fulfilled, at least not in a network.
- A second reason is the communicative power of PDCA-thinking. When decision-making and implementation are presented and communicated as the result of a PDCA cycle, this implies that the decision-making and implementation have been well thought out and systematically established. When decision-making and implementation are presented and communicated as the result of consultation and negotiation, the idea that they are the result of opportunism and coincidence could arise. However, anyone who thinks that this communicative power implies that PDCA can also be used for *real-world* decision-making in a network is mistaken. There is a difference between perception and reality. The communicative power of PDCA can be used strategically in a network. Process-based activity and project-based communication is an important strategy.

Implementation: new round, new opportunities

When parties have made a decision this decision can then be implemented. This could mean that the process-based approach loses significance and that the parties switch to project management. There is consensus regarding the need to implement the decisions, so nothing stands in the way of a project-based approach.

However, this is not necessarily always the case because the distinction between decision-making and the implementation of a decision, or series of decisions, is not always clear-cut. There are two reasons for this.

In the first place, implementation in a network partly comprises implementation of the package deal, but it is also partly made up of a new round of decision-making, with new opportunities for the parties' own interests to be achieved. So it is quite possible that during the 'implementation' there is a redefining of the problem definition or the goal, or new opportunities arise that demand a new decision. In a nutshell, the game of consultation and negotiation, of give and take, of linking and unlinking, can continue into the implementation phase, certainly when open-ended decisions have been made. The degree of freedom for renewed consultation will often be more limited than it was before the parties agreed to the package deal but not always.

In a project-based approach the decision-making process is likened to a funnel or is referred to as 'funnelling'. The degree of freedom the actors have decreases as the decision-making process progresses. Once the decision has been made, the funnel narrows and the actors' freedom is reduced even more. Further decisions should be implemented in conformance with the decision that was already made. The process-based approach is more like an hourglass: During the process from problem formulation to decision formulation, the actors' level of freedom doesn't decrease a great deal. They still have enough space for their consultation and negotiation processes. Then there is a narrowing: The parties compile a package of decisions and related agreements. After this decision-making the hourglass can once again widen. The implementation phase can lead to new negotiations.

Does this now mean that processes drag on and there are never concrete results? No, the package deal will always include decisions that lend themselves to project-based implementation. It is even possible that certain projects will be implemented before the formal decision has been made. When everyone is in agreement regarding such a project and nobody is scared that the implementation of such a project means that one of the parties will receive the profit too soon, there is no reason for delay.

In the second place, project-based logic assumes that first a decision in made and that this is then implemented. This doesn't have to be the case. When parties negotiate with each other about a multi-issue agenda, numerous links between issues are possible. Many of these links are made but never reach the formal decision-making phase. Parties make a link and then simply switch to action.

Take a university professor who is responsible for a particular subject. He teaches the subject twice a year and updates it every time: He adds the latest insights, uses new examples and tries to improve the electronic learning environment. After a number of years the subject looks very different due to the cumulative effect of all these changes. Has a formal decision regarding these changes ever been made by the director or the professor? No, this type of change is 'emergent'. Similar mechanisms also appear in the processes in networks. Parties take action without a decision having been made in advance. Suppose that all actions in organisations, between parties or in families required a formal decision. Life would probably grind to a halt in an enormous bureaucratic clatter.

Anyone who only looks at implementation through project-based glasses will very quickly become frustrated. Decisions are made – sometimes only after a long and tiresome process – and then a portion of the decisions are not implemented, but the game of consultation and negotiation appears to start all over again. Anyone who looks through process-based glasses sees that during the process parties are already carrying out activities that will never lead to formal decision-making but will deliver results. See the above example of the professor.

Decision follows action – circumvents formal decision-making

The above leads to the first strategy regarding implementation: Circumventing formal decision-making could be sensible because sometimes processes offer possibilities for parties to take collective action without a formal decision in advance being required. These parties can then achieve their interests in a simple way. If they wait for a formal decision before taking action, they run two risks: Their action will be delayed, and there is a chance that the proposal will not survive the formal decision-making unscathed. Decision-making implies that other parties will also focus on the intended action. This is risky, especially if it is not know in advance whether they will support this action.

Implementation is a new round, so it offers new opportunities

In project-based logic implementation can be defined as giving concrete form to the decision. As we have said, in a network this is often not the case. Certainly when decisions are not cut-and-dried but offer room for manoeuvring, implementation is a new round in the consultation and negotiation process and, therefore, offers new opportunities for the involved parties. They can try to redefine the decision, postpone implementation or implement the decision in a different way than was intended. In addition, new opportunities may arise that could require a totally different decision or the total reversal of the decision.

Actors in a network who know that implementation is 'only' a new round in the process can also anticipate this. Consultation and negotiation processes can involve considerable costs: Sometimes they cost a lot of time, and they can affect relationships with other parties even though there is no guarantee that they will lead to success. It can be attractive for actors to adopt a passive attitude in these processes with the knowledge that in the implementation phase there will still be sufficient space to achieve their own interests. An additional benefit could be that an actor who has adopted a passive attitude, and as a result has received very little profit, still has some credit with the

Table 4.5 Implementation in a project and in a process

Project-based decision-making	Decision making in networks
Implementation follows the decision.	The decision follows the already undertaken actions, or decision-making is circumvented.
Decision-making gives compulsory direction to the implementation.	Partial-result decision-making but also new rounds and new opportunities
Implementation is an operational activity.	Implementation requires strategic choices.

other parties. An actor who has made a lot of profit from the securing of the package deal may be less powerful when it comes to the implementation.

Implementation also demands strategic choices and creates points of no return

Actors with an interest in the implementation of a package of decisions will be apprehensive about a number of the aforementioned strategies. When a package of decisions has been recorded and other actors view the implementation as nothing more than a new negotiation round or try to unfreeze the decisions, this can adversely affect other parties' interests.

The risk of these strategies is limited if enough actors have an interest in the implementation being in line with the decisions. An actor who then tries to reopen negotiations puts his relationships with many other actors in the balance, which is not advisable in a network of repetitive interdependencies.

Another strategy is the creation of *points of no return* in the implementation process. Suppose it has been decided that a railway line will be laid between points A and B – a distance of two hundred kilometres. Thirty kilometres before B the line can run either via routes C or D. After lengthy negotiations it is decided that, despite considerable opposition, the line will go via C. The implementation of this decision can be defined as a strategic activity. Not waiting too long to start work on laying the track at C may be a good idea, even though, from an operational perspective, this may not be the most logical approach. Until construction work at C actually starts, there is a chance that discussions about the route will reopen. Track-laying at C will limit the possibilities of this happening because it has created a point of no return.

Evaluation: achieving a goal isn't everything

Finally there is the evaluation of the process. The crucial difference between a project-based approach and a process-based approach is that in a project-based approach evaluation is a goal-based activity. The most important question is whether the goals formulated in advance have been achieved (effectiveness) and what this cost (efficiency).

In a process-based approach this is not possible for a number of reasons:

- Different parties can have different goals and different opinions regarding whether goals have been achieved.
- Goals formulated *in advance* are not a guideline for an evaluation because parties can change their goals during the process. During a process parties can learn about their goals, the correct problem definition and the most suitable solution.
- Parties can also participate in a decision-making process without having a particular goal, which makes goal-based evaluation problematic.

- An evaluation is a snapshot. When different decision-making processes are linked to each other because a meaningful evaluation of decision-making process A cannot be formulated without considering the way it links with B, C and D?

When evaluating processes in a network, other criteria are relevant.

Are parties satisfied?

Question one is whether the parties are satisfied with the package deal. It's very possible that before the process began they had a number of (broad) goals but that during the process these goals changed and, despite this, they are very satisfied with the result. The tolerance criterion is also relevant: Although parties may not be satisfied, they tolerate the outcomes of a process either because the outcomes give them more profit than loss or because they will still need the other parties in the future and, for this reason, do not want to block a package deal.

Have problems been solved?

Question two is whether problems have been solved in the process. Not just the problems of the actor who initiated the decision-making but also the problems of other actors. A process may have started in order to do something about actor A's problem X, but if in hindsight it has contributed towards solving a problem of actor B, then the process has certainly been valuable. It could also be the case that the process has contributed towards solving problem Y of actor A but problem X has not been solved. Then too the process has contributed towards solving a problem, so everything does not revolve around the achievement of the problems formulated in advance by the initiator.

Have parties learned?

Question three is whether parties have learned during the process (Cross, 1977; Muthusamy & White, 2005). They have been confronted with new issues and information, and this could have led to them having a different standpoint. For example, a product development manager had believed there was a good market for new product A, but during the negotiations with other actors within the company, he learned that this is not the case and new product B is a far better prospect.

Suppose this manager's superiors work with a SMART evaluation system. The manager must state specific, measurable, acceptable, realistic and time-bound goals (targets) that are evaluated after one year. If the manager gives the introduction of product A as a goal, there are two risks: The Manager has bound himself to the achievement of A, so he is unable to learn anything, or he is willing to learn and opts for product B, in which case he runs the risk of being penalised with a bad evaluation.

Have enduring relationships been created?

This is the fourth important criterion. Are the parties willing to negotiate with each other again in a following round and in respect of other issues? Or have the negotiations been so laborious and has so much distrust been created that future cooperation is ruled out? This, too, is an aspect that is very important for decision-making in networks but that can be overlooked in classic evaluations. Suppose that goals are formulated in advance and are achieved but in such a way that the relationships with all the other actors have been so seriously damaged that every form of future cooperation is ruled out. And compare this with a situation in which goals haven't been fully achieved, but there is still ample scope for future cooperation. This second situation is preferable from a network perspective, but the first situation will do better in a strict project-based evaluation.

Has the process been fair?

The fifth criterion is whether the process has been conducted fairly (Hollander-Blumoff & Tyler, 2008). Have the participating parties had sufficient opportunities to achieve their interests? Have their core values been respected? Have their opinions been listened to? There is a possibility that parties are not completely satisfied with the result of the process but accept it because the process was conducted fairly and they realise that blocking the decision-making would do more harm than good.

Evaluation is an ongoing process

In a traditional project-based approach evaluation is the final phase of the project. In networks evaluation is far more an *ongoing process*. The participating parties will continuously assess whether they and others are satisfied with the interim results and the prospects for profit or whether learning processes are occurring or relationships are still good and whether the process is being conducted fairly. Evaluation has more the character of a continuous monitoring of the process than of a separate activity afterwards.

Table 4.6 Evaluation in a project and in a process

Project-based decision-making	*Process-based decision-making*
Have goals formulated in advance been achieved?	Are parties satisfied? Have problems been solved? Have parties learned? Have trusted relations for the future been created? Has the process been fair?
Evaluation is a post-project activity.	Evaluation is a continuous, process-monitoring activity.

If, despite the network-based character of the decision-making, a classic evaluation is carried out, the parties may set great store by a positive evaluation. There are, of course, incentives to manipulate this. The parties can agree that they will present and communicate the process as a project. They can blame certain results on the process, even if they came into being without a process. Perhaps during the decision-making they have already discussed how they will present the result of the process externally. (We call this *negotiated success*.) A positive evaluation is not the outcome of a neutral and analytical investigation, but – as is nearly always the case in a network – the result of agreements between parties.

The law of diminishing effectiveness

In this and the previous chapters we have talked about many strategies. We must remember that all of these strategies are subject to the law of diminishing effectiveness (Lees, 2005; Shephard & Färe, 1974). What this law means is that the effectiveness of a strategy can decrease after a time. The reason for this is simple: When a strategy has been used a number of times, other actors learn to recognise it and understand what its effect can be. They can then try to nullify the influence of the strategy by following counter-strategies. Examples of such counterstrategies are:

- Follow a strategy to the point of absurdity: If an actor designs a multi-issue agenda in order to create a multitude of coalitions, other actors can add so many issues to this agenda that the totality of issues becomes uncontrollable. The strategy has been pushed too far, so it loses its effectiveness.
- Point out the weak public performance of the strategy: Strategies are often less suitable for the public performance or frontstage. If an actor formulates a problem in broad terms in order to make it attractive for other actors, other actors can block the strategy by pointing out that the problem formulation would appear vague and ambiguous frontstage, which casts doubt on the usefulness of cooperation.
- Explain and expose the strategy: A strategy can also be robbed of its effectiveness by explaining and exposing it. If, for example, actor A compiles a multi-issue agenda, actor B's counterstrategy is to explain it: Rumour has it that the 'only' purpose of the multi-issue strategy is to achieve actor A's goal. When this perception is planted in the minds of other actors, there is less chance of them participating in the multi-issue game.

What does the law of diminishing effectiveness mean for a decision-making process?

In the first place it makes the decision-making process even more dynamic and erratic. It can definitely engender a chain of strategies and counterstrategies. Add all these strategies and counterstrategies together, and the result is an increased number of uncertainties and a less predictable outcome of the decision-making process.

A footballer who takes a penalty has a strategy: He has a favourite way of taking the shot. During the 1988 European Football Championship the Dutch goalkeeper, Hans van Breukelen, gained the reputation of being a penalty killer. How was his success explained; what was his strategy? The answer was 'Reker's little book'. For many years Jan Reker, a Dutch football trainer, watched how European top players took penalties and noted it down in a little book. His idea was that, caught up in the tension of a European tournament, when these players took a penalty they would rely on their routines, which meant he could predict how they would take the shot. Hans van Breukelen had access to 'Reker's little book'.

So, the effectiveness of a player's strategy (his favourite way of taking a penalty) decreases because, after a number of penalties, other players know your favourite way to shoot. It is the law of diminishing effectiveness. However, the dynamic continues. If a goalkeeper stops a penalty a number of times, other players, trainers and the media go looking for the explanation. At some point Hans van Breukelen's secret was reported in the newspapers. Now everyone knew about 'Reker's little book'. The goalkeeper's strategy no longer worked because the player taking the penalty now knew that Van Breukelen would respond to his favourite way of shooting, so he did it a different way. But the keeper can move on to the following strategy: He now knows the player knows he has 'Reker's little book'. Then the player knows that the goalkeeper knows that the player knows that the goalkeeper knows his favourite way of taking a penalty. It is the law of diminishing effectiveness in its optimum form. Nobody's strategic information is of any use to them now. It's time for a different strategy.

In the second place, every actor is, at some point, confronted with the law of diminishing effectiveness or with a chain of strategies and counterstrategies that create so much uncertainty that the effect of the strategy also diminishes. This means that management in networks demands continuous strategic innovation. Anyone who constantly relies on the same strategy loses his effectiveness. This is a major difference with project management. A project management handbook lasts a lifetime; the strategies in a network have a limited shelf life.

In the third place, the more an actor is bent on achieving his own interest, at least in the perception of the other actors, the sooner this law will be activated. Once again take the multi-issue decision-making strategy. It can be followed in two ways:

- *Prudently*: This means that an actor designs a multi-issue game purely with the aim of ensuring the decision-making is attractive for everyone. It means that during the exchange process that will follow, this actor will, if necessary, be willing to reformulate his own goals or even give them up.

- *Opportunistically*: This means that actor A follows a multi-issue strategy with the aim of getting other actors necessary for decision-making around the table. However, the purpose of the multi-issue agenda is not to organise an attractive exchange process for all the other actors but to increase the chances of actor A's goals being achieved. The other actors could, for example, be pressurised into participating.

Opportunistic behaviour leads to the other actors having incentives to rob the strategy of its effectiveness. When an actor behaves more prudently, these incentives will decrease. The strategy will then be followed but by taking into account the interests of these other actors. In other words, there are incentives for behaving prudently and moderately for anyone who wishes to invest in good, longer-term relationships and activate the law of diminishing effectiveness as little as possible. For a prudent and opportunistic way of using these strategies, see also Chapter 7.

5   Smart command and control

The disadvantages of process-based strategies

The previous chapters considered the strategies that work in an inter-connected world. Those who are familiar with these strategies will also be aware that they may also have significant disadvantages. The two most important of those are:

1   They may lead to outcomes the parties are dissatisfied with – to ugly, dreary, grey compromises. Friedrich Engels phrased this nicely as: '*Denn was jeder einzelne will, wird von jedem andern verhindert, und was herauskommt, ist etwas, das keiner gewollt hat*' ('What each individual wants is obstructed by everyone else, and what emerges is something that no one willed', Engels 1890). The parties have entered into a process; they learn that the exit option is no longer truly possible and have to arrive at a deal. However, nobody is really satisfied with that deal. Decisions within a process may sometimes come about with a great deal of difficulty – and it is then hard to introduce a compromise that nobody wants – back into the discussion. As Henry Kissinger puts it: 'Decisions taken with enormous doubt and perhaps with a close division become practically sacrosanct once adopted' (Johns, 1973) – the decision becomes sacrosanct, even if it does not, ultimately, suit anyone.

2   They may lead to cumbersome and suboptimal processes, taking up a significant amount of time and thereby losing their legitimacy. The economist Charles Lindblom once called this as 'muddling through' (Lindblom, 1959; Migone & Howlett, 2015; Morgan, 2016). Madeleine Albright referred to the decision-making process between the Americans, Palestinians and Israelis as 'herding cats' (Albright, 2003, p.317). The Irish saying for this is 'minding mice at a cross road'. The Germans talk about '*Weichkochen*' ('cooking until soft'): consulting and negotiating for so long that each actor has become punch-drunk and no longer has any clear or explicit opinions. The French have the expression '*noyer dans la soupe*': allowing things to boil for too long until the soup becomes a colorless and tasteless substance. The Flemish refer to it as endless

'*palaveren*' ('muttering'). These are all expressions of the frustration that is inherent to decision-making in a network: It takes too long.

These disadvantages are in part inevitable. It is the price parties pay to reach an agreement – and it is evident that they feel the price of substandard compromises and/or time-consuming processes are worth it for their agreement.

This chapter explores the question about which strategies are able to contribute to mitigating these disadvantages. Chapter 1 suggested that networks should be positioned in opposition to a hierarchy. Command and control is the dominant style within a hierarchy – a style which does not work at all within a network. However, this is not the whole picture – command and control does work in a network under certain conditions, and therefore, an actor can use the command-and-control style under these very specific conditions. This is referred to as 'smart command and control': the use of command and control where actors are conscious that they are in a network and only able to apply this strategy under specific conditions. Smart command and control may contribute to avoiding dull compromises or reducing the time decision-making takes.

When can command and control be applied in a network?

Several smart command-and-control strategies are presented in this section. An actor needs, of course, to have the means in place to be able to utilise a command-and-control strategy. For instance, an actor needs to have the ability to impose rules, to make funding available or withdraw it, to have a formal hierarchical role or to be able to evoke media power. Normally speaking, an actor in a network would have to apply this moderately: Applying these types of resources unilaterally leads to a significant risk of resistance by the other actors within the network – a unilateral intervention will rebound like a boomerang. However, there are a number of opportunities for using command and control where an actor has the means available.

Threatening command and control to influence other actors' perceptions of gain

Decision-making in networks has the greatest chance of success where there is a win-win situation. Every actor experiences a gain and loss, but for each one of these, the profit/loss balance ends up in the black: The profit is higher than the loss. Where this is the case, actors will be prepared to support the package deal: Those who do not will be putting their profit in the balance (Kickert, Klijn, & Koppenjan, 1997).

There is a significant risk of resistance when an actor suddenly applies a command-and-control strategy during the decision-making process. However, it is different when an actor only *threatens* command and control without implementing this threat. Threats such as these may influence actors' perceptions of their gain and loss.

A simple example may clarify this. Imagine there are two individuals, both forty years old, who are walking along together when one of them suddenly draws a pistol, aims at the other's chest and demands he hands over fifty euros. This is in essence a win-win situation: One of the parties receives fifty euros, the other forty years of additional life. So what is happening here? Aiming a pistol at another's chest is a command-and-control threat. The threat changes the perception of the situation of the person with the fifty euros. Without the threat, he would not, of course, ever have handed over the fifty euros – as there is nothing he would receive in return. Given there is now a threat of being shot, command and control influences the other actor's perception of the profit/loss ratio.

There are many examples of this strategy to be found in environmental policy (Woolley & McGinnis, 1999). In the nineties the European Commission (EC) announced it would impose unilateral standards for CO_2 emissions from cars. This influenced the perceptions of the car industry about their profit and loss. The profit for industry would rise should the EC back down from its intention to develop these standards unilaterally.

The EC appeared subsequently to be prepared to negotiate about these standards and concluded a voluntary agreement with the industry. This led to a win-win situation. The industry committed itself to a plan – a 'negotiated self-commitment' – for a reduction in emissions as well as to a system to monitor this. In exchange for this, the EC withdrew from unilateral standardisation. Had the EC not threatened unilateral standardisation then its negotiating position would have been significantly weaker (Commission of the European Communities, 2000).

The shadow of hierarchy: command and control may also be utilised where the process is not going to plan

Where the previous example talked about an active threat, there is also discussion of the idea of passive threat in the literature, which is referred to as the 'shadow of hierarchy' (Scharpf, 1997). In this instance there is no command-and-control intervention, yet the parties need to keep in mind that one could be applied. A *potential* application of command and control casts a shadow over the decision-making process. Avoiding the actual intervention becomes a form of profit for actors in the process.

An example of this is to be found in the agreements between the German government and the business world about the collection and reuse of batteries and the environmentally friendly processing of scrapped cars. The German government used the 'shadow of the law' in both sets of agreements: There were negotiations, but were the negotiations not to lead to a result, there was the threat that the government would implement rules unilaterally. In both situations, the 'shadow of the law' was an important incentive to arrive at the agreements voluntarily (Busch & Jörgens, 2001; Thatcher, 2004). The shadow of the law is a passive threat, which may also influence the other parties' perception of profit and loss.

Command and control as an incentive for a process

Command and control can be used as an incentive to get the process of consultation and negotiation started.

Imagine that an actor wants to get a large project off the ground that will affect the interests of a significant number of parties. The actor is keen to include these other parties in the decision-making. There are two ways in which the actor can attempt to get these parties around the table.

The first way is to invite the other parties without being entirely explicit about his own project. After all, the actor wants to be able to give these other parties the opportunity to exercise their influence. They are being invited, therefore, to participate in a process with a broad and open agenda. The risk of this approach is that the other actors will think the initiative too vague and will therefore not accept the invitation to arrive at a decision through a joint process. A broad and open agenda sometimes does not work: It does not capture the attention of the actors involved.

This was sharply underlined in a study about the creation of 'smart cities' – cities or districts with high-level information technology (IT) infrastructure and services (Weening, 2006). The initiative-taker adopted an open approach on the belief that this alone would bring about an interaction between the parties and that these parties would arrive jointly at a decision. However, this openness so early in the process led to such a great deal of uncertainty in the parties that too few parties were incentivised to join it.

The second approach is for the initiative-taker to opt for a command-and-control–like position. The other parties are unilaterally informed that the initiator intends to implement a project that affects the interests of the other parties. The other parties will immediately have to sit up and take notice, probably putting up resistance to the project. This benefits the initiative-taker, who will have the attention of the other parties. These other parties will now very likely accept the invitation to join the process that attempts to arrive a decision together.

Command and control is therefore an incentive for parties to enter a process. This strategy requires a strategy estimate: Will the parties contribute to the process, and will they be sufficiently cooperative? After all, anyone selecting command and control when presenting a project runs the risk that the other actors will be so irritated they are no longer prepared to collaborate in the process.

Command and control when a process of collaboration has failed

Consultation and negotiation processes may fail, yet is a failed process always a negative result? Not by definition. When parties in a negotiation process are not able to reach a consensus, this becomes the basis for command and control. A unilateral, hierarchical intervention will take place, but the wisdom lies in doing this *once* a process has failed.

A failed process may be fertile grounds for unilateral interventions, for at least two reasons.

First, actors negotiating with each other will *learn* during this process. They will learn that they are unable to reach a decision or package of decisions. This may then lead to two situations:

- They accept that no decisions will be made; or
- They become more open to other types of decision-making.

The stronger the feeling amongst the others that a decision is required and that *non–decision-making* is therefore not an option, the more receptive they will be to unilateral interventions – for command and control. This will lead to some loss, but the loss resulting from non–decision-making might be greater. A fair process that has failed may thereby promote the legitimacy of command and control once this process has finished (Kickert et al., 1997, pp.173–174). This legitimacy would be much more controversial should an actor have taken a unilateral decision without giving the process a chance.

Second, an actor applying command and control after a failed process has probably also learned during that process. The actor may have learned about positions: What are the parties' positions; where did potential coalitions arise; which parties are too far apart; and which parties approached each other during the process? The actor may also have learned about contents: What are the most important issues; what are the intrinsic differences in opinion; where do the experts have authoritative expertise; and which expertise is disputed? This knowledge acquired during the process may – if the process fails – be used in the design of a clever command-and-control strategy.

Command and control in terms of procedures

This refers to command and control being used to impose a procedure on actors, which they then need to follow in the decision-making process. The command and control 'only' relates to the procedure; it has no impact on the contents of the decision to be made.

This strategy may be attractive given that procedures are not neutral; they also partly determine the contents of the outcome. John Rawls gives the example of a cake to be divided up (Rawls, 1971). Imagine that party A has a cake and party B has a knife. Party A wishes to divide the cake between six people, including A and B, and wants everyone to receive the same size slice.

Were A to share his or her viewpoint unilaterally with B, there is every reason then to assume that B will not agree with A. B has an indispensable resource for A – a knife – and probably therefore should be rewarded for this with a larger slice of cake. B knows that A is dependent on B and will view A's stance – same size slice of cake for everyone – as the first step in the negotiations. Or B may be so irritated by A's stance that B walks away in search of another party with a cake.

A unilateral intervention by A may also be procedural. A may inform B that he does not want to be involved in the size of the cake slices, so he explains a procedure to B: B must cut the cake into six slices; he is allowed to decide for himself how large each cake slice is; but as a result, he has to choose the last slice. It is this procedure that forces B to cut equal-sized slices. There is, after all, a significant risk of B receiving the smallest slice of cake.

Procedures may significantly affect the outcome of a process – and, therefore, it may be in one actor's interest to impose procedures via command and control. There is another advantage to this: There is a large risk of resistance when an actor imposes an intrinsic viewpoint on others. Resistance against procedures is less straightforward. It may be perceived by others as a bureaucratic attitude focused solely on the content. Resistance against procedures is not attractive, meaning there is an opportunity for imposing these unilaterally on the other party in the network.

Now in the example of the cake, the procedure was highly impactful on the outcome. It is likely that B would have seen through A's intervention and not agreed to the procedure. Procedures may also be used to minimise the risk of undesirable outcomes: There may be no certainty about the outcome, but there is certainty that an undesirable outcome is nearly impossible. Rawls refers to criminal law procedures as an example. An undesirable outcome is that the innocent are convicted. All kinds of *checks and balances* have therefore been introduced into procedures to prevent judicial errors: between the police and the public prosecution service, between the public prosecution service and the judge and between the district court, the court of appeal and the Supreme Court. The procedures minimise the risk of undesirable outcomes.

Regret minimisation: command and control, but offering space at the same time

Command and control can go hand in hand with offering space. An actor can use the command-and-control strategy on the one hand and offer space on the other. We will describe an example in the first instance and then discuss the wisdom behind this.

Imagine a board of directors intends to merge two divisions. The divisions are powerful players in the organisation and have a high degree of autonomy and are therefore difficult to steer. Furthermore, there is a great deal of resistance within both divisions against the idea of a merger.

Imagine now that the board of directors invites both divisions to explore through a process of consultation and negotiation whether to work more collaboratively or even whether a merger is desirable. There is a significant chance that this process will lead to nothing. The divisions simply have no interest in a merger. As the saying goes, there is no prize for guessing the outcome when the turkey is invited to discuss Christmas dinner: The chance of *filet de dinde* being on the menu is exceptionally small.

Command and control will therefore have little chance of success given the positions of power of both divisions. To put it more emphatically, command and control will be an incentive for them to form a coalition with the aim of blocking the decision.

Command and control may offer a consolation here if it is paired up with offering space to both sides. Suppose that the board of directors takes the unilateral decision that both divisions need to merge – a form of command and control. Suppose next that the board of directors pairs this up with some space: The newly merged division will be allowed to submit proposals for the organisational structure and strategy. What could be the wisdom behind such a strategy?

The divisions are faced with a tricky decision: Resist the merger, or accept the merger and use the space offered as much as possible. The latter may be an attractive option. The space can, after all, be used to design an organisational structure for the new division, consisting of the two former divisions, each with a great deal of autonomy. This strategy may stipulate that the activities of the old divisions remain independently recognisable. These are attractive options for the two divisions.

Suppose, though, that despite this space the choice is made to resist, what are the associated risks?

First, it is tricky to direct this resistance. The alternative – using the space – is after all attractive, and the risk of staff in the divisions changing tack is always present. The resistance will soon crumble once this starts to happen. More than that, it may be attractive for staff to be the first to report to the board of directors that they are accepting the offer. Those first staff will, perhaps, gain the most – the principle of 'the first winner takes all'. When the perception of 'the first winner takes all' sets in with staff in the two divisions, there is a significant chance that resistance will very quickly crumble.

Secondly, the mechanism of regret minimisation arises. Suppose that the space is not used but that the resistance also crumbles, then the chance arises that the divisions, viewing things retrospectively, will regret refusing to cooperate. Had they cooperated from the start, they would have the maximum degree of freedom. There is a considerable risk that, should they not cooperate and the resistance crumbles, the board of directors would limit the degree of freedom. The board of directors is able to utilise this by indicating that the level of freedom may be reduced if the divisions don't cooperate. The divisions will want to minimise their regret in retrospect and perhaps agree to the merger.

Thirdly, the divisions will have another interest in addition to maintaining their independence: sustaining a good relationship with the board of directors. The board has made them an offer, therefore they will have to play along in the give-and-take game and make a move at the very least. Anyone who believes that any restriction on the autonomy of their own division is nonnegotiable is not playing along in the game of give and take and is therefore putting his relationship with the board in the balance.

The good and bad guy with the command and control approach

A variation on this is the 'good guy/ bad guy' strategy (Brattström & Richtnér, 2014; Fili, 2014). An actor allows himself to be represented by two people, one of whom has the role of the 'bad guy' who adopts a command-and-control:

- like approach, continuously threatening unilateral interventions and therefore seeking confrontation with the other actors. The other person takes a more cooperative approach: They are focused on consultation and want to respect the interests of the other actors and create a win-win situation. Threats from the bad guy may strengthen the good guy's position. The others, under the influence of the threat from the bad guy, will perhaps redefine their perception of gain. Or they may become more receptive to the good guy's wishes, in order to be safeguarded from interventions by the bad guy. Should the other actors suggest that a command-and-control
- like approach does not fit with networks and that parties should arrive at a decision or package of decisions through fair consultation, good guys are always able to claim that they are looking for fair consultation.

Command and control when there is a critical mass of winners

During a process actors attempt to design a package of decisions that creates a win-win situation for each of themselves. What happens during this process when a party concludes that the gains have been achieved and that a win-win situation has been created for them? This party will want to move to a definitive decision. After all there is a chance that the gains will be lost if the process is continued.

A critical mass of winners may arise at any moment in the process: parties who have achieved their gains and want to move to a definitive decision. An actor who consequently applies a command-and-control strategy and states that a decision needs to be taken – and that the time for negotiation has past – will in all likelihood count on a lot of support, even if there are still actors who have not yet seen sufficient gains.

The extent of the critical mass is difficult to quantify and objectify. It depends, amongst other things, on the power of the relevant party and their numbers, as well as the degree to which they are passionate about their gains. Are they extremely passionate about the gains and therefore want to move to a decision, or are they less passionate, open to a potential further postponement in the decision?

Why is it not very productive for actors who have not yet seen sufficient gains to resist the decision-making process? Because by doing so they put the gains of the large majority of actors in the balance. The interdependencies of these actors are recurrent: They will meet each other again in the future, and anyone putting the relationship with a large number of actors in the balance runs the risk of reputational damage – and reputational damage may negatively affect future cooperation. Therefore, for those actors who are not part of the critical mass of winners, it is not just a question of profit and loss within this decision-making process: It is also about which loss will lead to a blockage in decision-making in subsequent processes.

This mechanism occurs in numerous decision-making processes. The European Union (EU) has utilised the unanimity rule for a very long time. One member state could block a proposal against the wishes of all other member states. Anyone who knows this rule may be surprised that the EU is ever able to arrive at formal decisions. There will, after all, always be a member state opposed to a proposal who is, therefore, able to apply its right to veto. However, when a proposal is accepted by a critical mass of member states, then it is very tricky to target this with a veto. It blocks a large number of decisions and affects relations with numerous other member states. The former Dutch prime minister, Ruud Lubbers once referred to this as: 'if a dominant coalition develops that has reached consensus about a particular subject, the other member states are expected to "join the consensus"' (Andersson & Mol, 2002, pp.58–59).

Radiating success: command and control in public performance

The previous chapter discussed the distinction between 'backstage' and 'frontstage'. Backstage decision-making is network-like: It is characterised by consultation and negotiation, giving and taking, linking and uncoupling. This type of decision-making is imperative within a network in which actors are mutually dependent. However, on the frontstage the decision-making is being presented as if everything is running according to the ideal, project-like model: transparent, steps in the right order, linear.

The game of consultation and negotiation, giving and taking, linking and uncoupling has to be played, but its power of communication is limited. The game is associated with backrooms, opportunism and politicised approaches. It may be sensible, therefore, to act in a process-like manner but communicate in project-like terms.

This takes us back to the distinction for a second time. The game of consultation and negotiation takes place on the backstage; the decision or package of decisions is the result of this process. However, on the frontstage the decision can be presented as the result of command and control. This may make a significant impression on the parties who do not know or did not participate in the process. Suppose an actor, despite the numerous parties and interests, is able to intervene effectively in a unilateral manner. This may set into operation a mechanism referred to as: 'reflected glory': radiating success and contributing to a good reputation. An actor who in others' perception is powerful may make use of this. The actor may, for instance, be an attractive partner for others, enabling him or her to expand his relationship network. The actor may also be an attractive partner in a subsequent decision-making process.

The process with other actors may even lead to agreement about who may present the result as a command-and-control intervention. Ironically, this may be on condition that the actor allowed to do so provides something extra to the other parties during negotiations,

The wisdom of command and control in a network

What are the communal aspects of these command-and-control strategies summarised in the box below? There are three patterns to be discerned.

1	Threatening command and control in order to influence other actors' perception of gain – an active threat
2	The shadow of hierarchy: command and control may also be utilised when the process is not going to plan
3	Command and control as an incentive for a process
4	Command and control, when collaboration has failed
5	Command and control in terms of procedures
6	Regret minimisation: command and control but offering space at the same time
7	The good and bad guy with the command-and-control approach
8	Command and control when there is a critical mass of winners
9	Radiating success: command and control in public performance

The first pattern is that command and control *promotes* the process of interaction. Command and control stimulates a process. This pattern may be seen in strategies 1, 2 and 3. For these strategies command and control is followed by a process, and without this command and control there probably have been no, or a less-effective, process.

A second pattern is that there are opportunities for unilateral action as a *conclusion* to the process. This pattern is found in strategies 4, 5 and 8. Command and control is possible in a network but only thanks to the process.

A third pattern is that command and control simultaneously applies consultation on the one hand and negotiation on the other: strategies 5, 6 and 7. Command and control and consultation and negotiation are therefore linked in parallel.

In all cases, therefore, the chance of command and control succeeding will depend on whether it stands in one way or another in relation to the other style: a process of consultation and negotiation. It is embedded in more interactive forms of decision-making – in other words it is smart command and control. It is, of course, important that none of these strategies work by definition – there will always have to be an estimate of whether the strategy has a chance of success in the specific context within which the actor finds himself.

Principal and agent: the tension between project- and process-like strategies

There is also an important second question associated with the tension between command and control on the one hand and more process-like strategies on the other.

An example might help to introduce this question. Suppose that a mayor has an idea to make his city more environmentally friendly. Part of this plan is that 5000 additional trees are to be planted, 1250 trees every year for four successive years.

The mayor defines this initiative as a classic project – and delegates the implementation to one of his staff. This staff member gets to work and quickly learns that planting trees is less straightforward than it looks. In certain districts, many inhabitants are against the planting of trees, as they lead to more shadows across apartment complexes. The utility companies have problems with this, due to the large number of underground cables that could become damaged by the trees. Safety is an important issue in the town. In certain parts of the town trees have been felled recently to provide better viewpoints and therefore increased security. Certain parts of the town are designated as protected townscape – and therefore no trees may be planted there. Many politicians are opposed to this – saying it is token politics, the mayor's political toy. And so the list goes on. It is apparent that there are many parties involved in this initiative who are against the trees being planted.

What is going on here? Table 1.1 in Chapter 1 may help explain this. The mayor defines the situation he finds himself in as a hierarchy. He can instruct his staff member to plant the five thousand trees via command and control. To him this is a structured problem. The problem is that the town is not environmentally friendly enough and that the five thousand trees are a solution to this. Where there is a hierarchy and a structured problem, the implementation of the chosen solution becomes a simple project – define goals, make plans and implement the project.

Figure 5.1 outlines the tension. There is a principal and an agent. The principal defines the issue as a project, but in the agent's experience it is a process. If something does not go right – in the example less than 1250 trees are planted in a given year – the principal will react to this from a project-like mind set: more command and control and more precise planning. From the agent's perspective, this will only increase the problems – where he to put more pressure on the actors involved and define the plans more closely, this would only reinforce resistance. The agent therefore becomes trapped between the principal and the actors in the process.

It is important to think of this tension as, in essence, entirely natural. The mayor is at the top of the municipal organisation with a formal hierarchical structure. The mayor, as principal, is potentially responsible for hundreds of initiatives. Were he to define all of these as a process – all therefore with, in theory, unintended outcomes – he would completely lose control over the initiatives. By defining these as a project, he is able to keep better control of

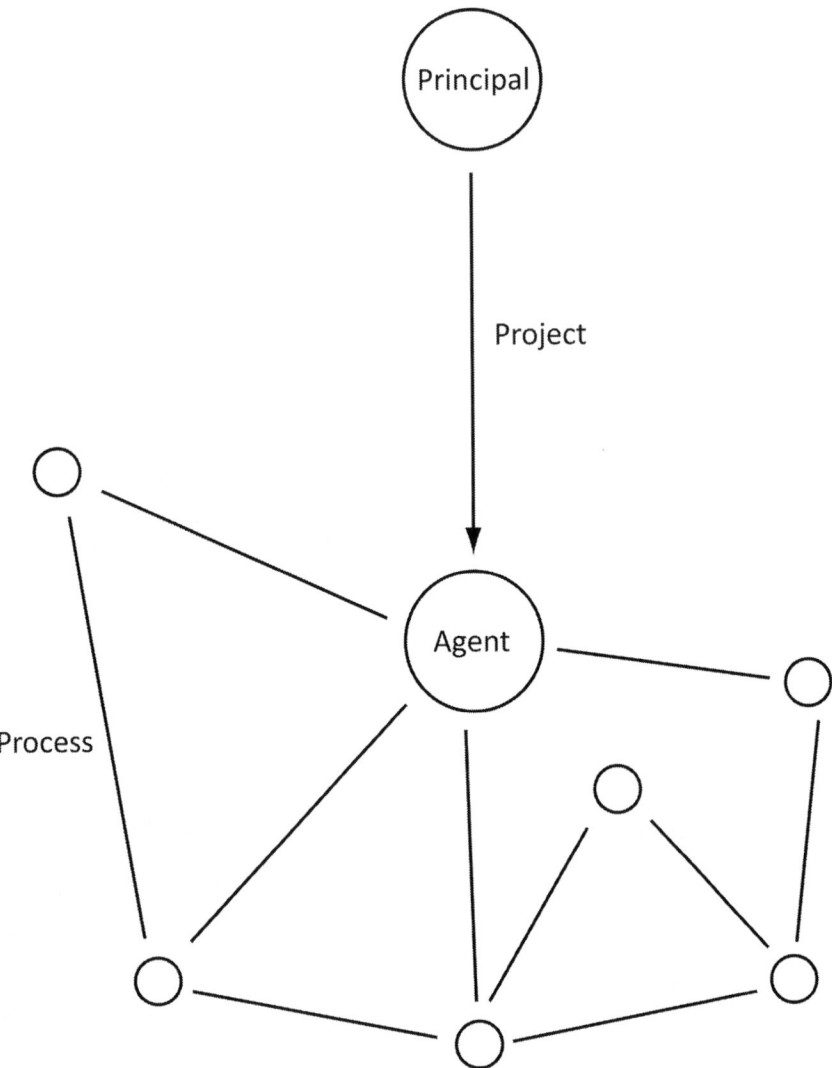

Figure 5.1 Principal and agent: project management versus process management

the initiatives – at least in his perception. A number of initiatives will also be actual projects. A number of others may perhaps be processes, but by defining them as projects, he is forcing the agents into potentially more disciplined behaviour than in a process. In the tree example: Perhaps the staff member concerned is being forced through the mayor's project approach into behaving more strictly towards those actors who are opposed to the idea –a smart use of more command and control. This may work. A third category of initiatives will appear in practice to be like a process – and this will lead to tension between principal and agent.

Because the principal's project-like approach is often natural behaviour, it makes little sense for the agent to demand the principal adopt a different approach. This is not about right and wrong – the agent is in the right and the principal in the wrong – it is more about a dilemma. The principal's position, and that of the agent, are understandable. A more fruitful question, therefore, is: Which strategies are available to the agent to deal with the tension?

Justifying the contents as well as the process

The agent finds himself in a hierarchical relationship to the principal and, therefore, must be able to justify himself at any point: Have the goals been attained, have they been attained on time and attained at as low a cost as possible? This justification is primarily based on contents; it is about results. In terms of the green project: Has the agreed-upon number of trees been planted?

What happens when an agent needs to realise objectives in a network – and therefore within a process with actors who are partly resistant to these goals? It is almost inevitable that the ultimate goal realisation will be a different one to that required by the principal.

One strategy for the agent is to make the principal aware of the reality of the network – of the dependencies and the actors' resistance and, therefore, for the need for the agent to play the decision-making game. This allows the agent not only to justify the intrinsic results of this game but also to justify the process: the way in which he played the decision-making game.

Using the latter, he will attempt to convince the principal of the quality of his efforts, particularly if there are seemingly meagre results. Meagre results may be the only possible outcome, after all, given the power relationships in a network.

This expands the justification playing field (see Table 5.1).

As shown in Table 5.1, justification may lead to the following four situations:

Good process, good result: The staff member has been able to plant the trees, and actors involved are happy with the process – the way in which they were involved in the decision-making about the planting of the trees.

Table 5.1 Accountability, content and process

	Justification for the process: The process was good	*Justification for the process: The process was poor*
Justification for the contents: The intended result was realised	Good process, good result	Poor process, good result
Justification for the contents: The intended result was not realised	Good process, poor result	Poor process, poor result

Good process, poor result: The agent was confronted with a lot of resistance, played the decision-making game well but unfortunately was unable to achieve a good result. Fewer trees were planted than planned.

Poor process, good result: The trees were planted – there are now five thousand trees in the municipality. However, this was associated with a lot of resistance – and many citizens are still furious about the trees which, in their opinion, have been forced on them by the council.

Poor process, poor result: The agent did not involve the actors concerned enough in the decision-making. This irritated them so much that they did their utmost to resist the tree planting. Both the result and the process were poor.

The idea is that this kind of justification makes the principal aware of the decision-making process and therefore leads to less stringent or more nuanced decisions, should this process not lead to the intended result. For instance, if the result was good, but the process poor, how would this affect the mayor? The consequence of this is that the citizens would have a lot of mistrust in the mayor. This may be very difficult the next time the mayor needs support from the local community – his or her relationship with the community has, after all, not improved. Or suppose that trees have been planted somewhere resulting in a road that has become less safe for school pupils going out in the evening. And suppose that something happens one time: a number of children have an accident. The mayor – who rushed his ideas through and organised the process so poorly – will be held accountable for all of this.

Including the principal in the consultation and negotiation process

A second strategy is for the agent to attempt to include the principal in the consultation and negotiation process with the actors in the network. This may come about by regularly informing the principal about progress in the process: How are the actors' views developing? What other issues do they want to include in the agenda? How much are they supporting the principal's goals? What strategic behaviours are they displaying? And so on.

Informing the principal and therefore including the principal in the decision-making has a number of benefits.

Information leads to learning: By informing the principal about progress in the decision-making, he will become aware of opportunities and lack of opportunities to realise his original goals. He will, for instance, learn that implementation is possible but only at a very high cost. Or he will learn of the opportunity to realise numerous other goals during the process. These types of learning process may lead to the principal redefining his original goals.

Information leads to commitment: Providing information appears to be a mild intervention: The agent is 'only' providing the principal with information about progress in the process. However, information often leads to commitment. If the principal is aware of the progress in a process but does not intervene, the principal apparently approves of the progress. When the outcomes do not suit the principal, or he or she is dissatisfied with the progress, the principal is partly responsible for this. When the principal is aware of the progress in the process and does intervene, the principal often becomes committed to the process. Dissatisfaction with progress or with the result may then also partially be attributed to the principal.

Information is managing expectations: If the principal is not included in the decision-making process, then he is able to maintain his original goals, and the result of the decision-making can only ever be disappointing to him. One thing is certain, however, in a network: The outcome of a process will always deviate from the parties' original intention. Including the principal is a form of expectation management: By keeping the principal informed, his expectations of the outcome will become more realistic.

Dilemma-sharing

One important strategy when including a principal in the decision-making processes is *dilemma-sharing* (Klijn, Edelenbos, Kort, & van Twist, 2008). This involves presenting the progress in the process in the form of dilemmas. An example of a dilemma is: 'If we opt to full goal realisation, then this will lead to actor C blocking another goal that is important to us. If we opt to go along with actor C, then we will not be able to realise our goals in full.'

What is the power of sharing dilemmas? Firstly, it allows us to see the complexity of processes in networks. Each solution has dis-benefits, and every solution, therefore, is sub-optimal. By formulating a situation as a dilemma, it becomes very difficult for the principal to fully maintain a project-like approach. There is a significant risk that the dilemma will lead to the principal being prepared to make a *trade-off* between his stance and that of other actors.

Secondly, there is something in the psychology of dilemma-sharing: By sharing a dilemma, the agent is targeting the principal's skills and competencies. Compare this with a situation in which the agent attempts to define the actors' resistance as a problem. Problems can irritate the principal: The agent is there to solve these problems; an unworkable situation arises when everyone presents their problems to the principal. By presenting a situation as a dilemma, the agent is suggesting that this is more than just an ordinary problem. The situation is apparently so complicated that it requires the principal's skills and competencies.

Making process agreements with actors in the network about what to do when there is no agreement from the principal

The agent is able to share his problem with the other actors in the network. He may suggest that agreement between him and the parties in the network may not by definition receive support from the principal. It is in no one's interest for the principal to block the agreement. It might, therefore, be sensible for the actors in the network and the agent to reach a number of process agreements in the event that this situation arises. These agreements may, for instance, mean that they reenter into mutual negotiations.

A minister may often have to negotiate with market players. For instance, students in the Netherlands have a public transport card. They are able to travel free of charge and choose from a number of different types of card, such as a weekly card, a weekend card or a weekly card combined with a discount card for the weekend. The minister of education concluded a contract for this with public transport companies in the Netherlands.

Suppose that the existing contract comes to an end and that the minister of education needs to renegotiate with the public transport companies. The question is whether the card scheme will be offered again to students and if so, what type of card and at what price. The education minister is accountable to parliament. He or she needs to receive approval from parliament for the outcome of the negotiations, and parliament is able to reject the result. Parliament is therefore the principal and the minister is the agent.

The minister is able to present the negotiating partners – the national railway companies and large bus firms – with these issues: The deal they conclude with the minister may be rejected by parliament, but the parties may consequently reach a process agreement. For instance, should the principal (in this example parliament) not approve the outcome of the negotiations, then this becomes a joint problem and the negotiation process resumes. Agreements such as this may be beneficial to all parties concerned:

- For the education minister as agent since rejection by parliament would not be exclusively his problem, which if it were would weaken the minister's position in negotiations;
- For public transport companies as actors in the network, who would still have the option of renegotiating following a rejection; and
- For parliament as the principal, it has more room to reject the outcome of the negotiations between the minister and the public transport companies since no serious problem will arise immediately as a result of doing so.

This type of process agreement provides for all parties around the negotiating table room and facilitates their negotiations. It brings about a comfortable environment. Consider the pressure that would arise on the negotiations had these process agreements not been reached. Without process agreements, the minister needs to achieve a result that will be accepted by parliament. This will be an incentive for the minister to adopt a hard and demanding approach because the minister wants to be sure that parliament will accept the outcomes of the negotiations. A hard and demanding approach, however, might damage the relationships with the negotiation partners.

These process agreements have another effect which arises during negotiations. Once negotiations are underway, it is of great importance for the parties to avoid these going on endlessly, with the principal (here: parliament) constantly rejecting the outcomes. There are incentives, therefore, to obtain the principal's approval.

This is something we often come across in negotiations: Process agreements are reached that serve to create a comfortable environment for the parties, particularly at the start of negotiations. However, during the negotiating process it is in the parties' interest to use the options offered by these agreements (concluding an accord, rejection by the principal and then renegotiation) as little as possible.

Using the principal's position as leverage for actors in the network

Another strategy is for the agent to make use of a situation where there is a project-minded principal rather than defining it as a problem. The agent can turn the principal's position and views into leverage against the other actors. The information available to the actors in the network is that the principal has a viewpoint, and any outcome from the negotiations that deviate from this will have little chance of success. A number of forms of smart command and control described in the first section of this chapter may be used for this, such as for instance the principal's position as the 'shadow of hierarchy' or as the incentive in the process. In particular, threatening to use command and control might be very effective. The agent may threaten a command-and-control intervention by the principal if actors in the network do not cooperate with him. There are two options the agent may provide, which together lead to four types of threat (see Table 5.2):

- Will the threat come from the agent or from the principal?
- Is there room for the actors in a network or no room?

The agent threatens, no room: This is not a very attractive option for an agent. The other parties will start to view him as an unreliable partner – someone who intimidates instead of negotiating. The threat can be a strong incentive to the other parties to intensify their resistance, particularly if the agent is not offering any room for manoeuvring.

The agent threatens, there is room: This is more attractive – there is room. However, the agent runs the risk that others will lose confidence in

Table 5.2 Four types of threat

	No room: *hard coercion*	Room: *soft coercion*
Direct threat: **own threat**	'If you don't agree with my proposal, I will implement rules'.	'I intend to implement the rules. Negotiate with me. If we arrive at a good agreement, I will not implement the rules'.
Indirect threat: **a third-person threat**	'If you don't agree to my proposal, my superiors will implement rules'.	'My superior wants to implement rules. Negotiate with me. If we arrive at a good agreement, my superior will not implement the rules'.

him. A negotiation partner who suddenly starts to threaten is not an attractive negotiation partner.

The principal threatens, no room: This is more appealing to the agent – the threat cannot be attributed to him. However, there is no room for the other actors – the risk of resistance therefore remains.

The principal threatens, there is room: This is perhaps the most appealing option for the agent. The threat cannot be attributed to him. There is room for negotiations. The message to the actors in the network could be that negotiating with the agent is an appealing option, and it pays to conclude a deal with the agent. This could mean the threat from the principal could be avoided.

Making it explicitly clear to the principal what the damage of rejecting the outcome of the negotiations is

When the principal sticks rigidly to his goals, this may lead to all types of damage:

- *Positional damage*: The relationship with the other actors in the network become severely disrupted, making future collaboration difficult.
- *Reputational damage*: When the principal brushes aside the actors in the network, this affects his reputation with these actors. They may perhaps see the principal as unreliable, as he is not bothered about their interests. The actors in the network may extend this image throughout their networks, meaning that the impact of this unreliability extends further than just these actors.
- *Intrinsic damage*: Actors learn during processes in networks. They exchange information and ideas and may change their original goals and views. A principal sticking to his goals will not be able to learn properly, and he may perhaps let chances go by.

During the process the agent may outline to the principal the damage that would be caused should he maintain his original goals. There is a chance that the principal might move by making this explicit. In addition to this it is often the case that a principal also has a principal – the next echelon in his organisation, a board of officers, a supervisory board, or the parliament. Should the risks become manifest, then the principal could be accused of having been warned of the risks yet knowingly taken them – something his superiors would not appreciate. This may have an effect on the degree to which the principal is sensitive to the agent's warnings.

Let's provide an example. Suppose that the minister for the environment is of the opinion that the waste issue in the Netherlands is so severe that waste disposal needs to be restricted. The minister formulates an objective to replace one-off packaging for consumer products as much as possible with multi-use packaging, which provides less waste. The carton boxes for milk need to be replaced by glass or polycarbonate bottles; the carton box for fruit juice also needs to be replaced with glass bottles; packaging for jams also needs to be transformed from one-off to multi-use glass.

The minister is the principal, and the officials charged with implementing this policy are the agents. The officials will, of course, consult with the most important market players. This includes a large number of individuals: packaging producers, the providers (producers of milk, juices, etc.), transport companies, the shop chains, consumer organisations, environmental organisations, etc. Suppose now that, as a result of this consultation, they arrive at the conviction that this switch from one-off to multi-use packaging is a disastrous policy:

- Intrinsic: The gains to the environment are limited; greater gains to the environment can be made elsewhere, and the costs of this switch are so high that the policy is not cost-effective.
- Positional: The proposed policy has incurred so much resistance in the business world that it becomes difficult for the environment minister to realise other reforms of policy for which he is also responsible.

The essence of the strategy of 'returning damage' is that officials make it explicitly clear to the minister what damage the proposed policy could incur.

By making this damage explicit, the officials are able to put the minister under pressure to be more sensitive to the opinions of the market players. There are two risks that arise if the minister sticks to his or her guns:

- Intrinsic and positional risks arise. The minister is stuck with a policy that is difficult to explain and which is also creating a great deal of resistance. Relationships with market players have been disrupted.

– Parliament (the minister's principal) may criticize him because the policy had negative effects and relationships with market players have been disrupted, even though the minister had been warned regularly about the potential for this to happen.

This is not a very appealing outlook for the minister and may be a reason for him to move to adopt a more flexible approach towards the parties in the network.

Implementing the principal's instructions

A variant of this strategy is one where the agent needlessly implements the principal's instructions. The agent does precisely what the principal demands of him. This may possibly lead to the abovementioned damage, but as the agent has done nothing more than implement the principal's instructions, all of this falls at the latter's door.

Activating the actors in the network

A strategy closely associated with the previous ones is where the agent utilises relationships with the actors in the network to influence his principal. The actors in the network perhaps will be in discussion with the principal about other issues or have relationships with actors who are in good standing with the principal or who may be superior to him. Through these relationships the principal may be informed about the viewpoints of the actors in the network and about the threatened intrinsic, positional and relational damage. This may be an appealing position for the agent, as he no longer has to be the bearer of bad timings.

Take, for instance, the example of parliament, the minister for education and the public transport companies. The minister is the agent, parliament the principal. When the minister has reached an agreement with the public transport companies, he may agree with them to use their influence to bring about an approval by parliament. The public transport companies may, perhaps, enjoy a good reputation with members of parliament – they may potentially be more sensitive to their views, rather than to the minister's.

Like it or lump it

A less elegant strategy the agent is able to use is for him to set out the outcome of the negotiations to his principal and for the principal to like it or lump it. In other words, there is a choice between either accepting the outcome of the negotiation or having no outcome at all.

To the principal this, of course, is an unappealing proposal, but it may be difficult to settle for no result when, for instance, there is a strong 'sense of urgency': This problem needs to be solved as quickly as possible. It may also be difficult to reject the outcome if this leads to a potential conflict between the principal and other players in the network. Suppose, for instance, that the agreement has been concluded after long-running negotiations and consultation with the most relevant actors. The costs of rejecting an outcome may then be very high. Rejecting the outcome not only results in a conflict with the agent but also with the actors involved.

Expanding the issue

Finally, there is a strategy that has been referred to a lot in this book: expanding the issue. To return once more to the example of the mayor and the trees: There will be more subjects at play between the mayor and staff than the trees alone. If the staff member is busy with other files, he could, of course, use these in the game with the mayor. Suppose that he is also busy with the new ring road around the municipality and with air quality in it. And suppose that he meets with some of the same actors as for the five thousand trees project. He can then link the subjects together. Problems with the trees could have consequences for the behaviour of actors in terms of the ring road and air quality. Or, the mayor should be aware that he really needs this staff member for the ring road and air quality – and therefore should not seek too many conflicts with him or her. The principal expends the issues and in doing so makes the agent aware that he must behave towards the agent in a reasonable yet authoritative manner.

Three footnotes

As for every strategy in networks, three footnotes need to be included for each of these strategies.

The first footnote is that each strategy requires an estimate of the power position of the actors in a network. 'Like it or lump it' will only work if the agent has sufficient authority in respect to the principal. Something similar to this applies to the strategy 'Activate the actors in the network'. If the agent's position of strength is insufficient, this strategy may lead to the actors in the network negotiating directly with the principal and the agent incurring reputational damage.

An extension of this is that strategies always give rise to contra-strategies, and the totality of strategies and contra-strategies may provide an unpredictable dynamic. The agent should therefore always be aware of this. The strategy 'Use the principal's position as leverage for the actors in the network' may lead to unpredictable and undesirable reactions, for instance, that the actors leave the negotiating table and start to consult with the agent's rival. Therefore, there is always the question of whether the agent has sufficient options to neutralise effects such as these.

The second footnote is that these strategies are subject to the law of diminishing effectiveness. Both the principal and the actors in the agent's network will recognise the strategy at any moment and reduce its impact. An agent who always uses the principal as leverage in negotiations may hereby incentivise actors in the network to develop or utilise informal relationships with the agent, meaning that this strategy becomes less effective over time.

Third, there is also the risk here that these strategies affect the agent's reliability. A minister is not able to function if he does not enjoy a good relationship with parliament. When agents consequently activate the actors in one network to influence members of parliament, that may affect the agents' reliability and thereby the minister's trust in them.

6 Strategic behaviour

Is using process-based strategies a bad thing?

In this book we have paid a lot of attention to the characteristics of networks and have shown that these characteristics impede linear, project-based decision-making. Decision-making in networks will only be successful if the inter-dependent multi-actor configuration is accepted as a fact. This demands more process-based strategies.

These strategies were reviewed in the preceding chapters, but these strategies, too, are not always undisputed. The strategic behaviour of parties – the way in which they play the game – can also invoke resistance. Sometimes actors do not tell the whole truth, are not explicit regarding their goals, tell a different story during their public performance than they did backstage, think of solutions first and then go looking for problems – the list could go on. Sometimes the behaviour appears opportunistic or even immoral and dishonest. Actors who behave strategically appear to be focused solely on their own interests rather than on the collective interest. This chapter is all about this strategic behaviour of actors – what it is in essence and how we should (or could) evaluate it normatively.

What is strategic behaviour?

Strategic behaviour is surrounded by a shroud of secrecy. Actors who behave strategically will work vigorously for their own interest. Sometimes they do it so cleverly and intelligently that they are able to keep it hidden – they strive for their own interest under the guise of collective interest. As a lot of strategic behaviour takes place in the back room and not in public, it is often unseen. This makes it difficult to assess how important strategic behaviour really is in practice and what influence it has on the decision-making (Heuvelhof, 2016).

There are writers who maintain that strategic behaviour is ubiquitous (Schelling, 1978), but this can also be relative. To a great extent it depends on which definition of strategic behaviour is used: Is every little white lie strategic behaviour? Every courteous phrase that doesn't entirely reflect the truth? Every exaggeration?

Others maintain that strategic behaviour has considerable *impact*. This line of reasoning inflates strategic behaviour into a root-cause explanation of decision-making outcomes that are seen as undesirable or irrational. Outcomes of decision-making that deviate from a 'rational' model become, as the *lender of last resort*, attributed to strategic behaviour (Flyvbjerg, 2007). That will also be an exaggeration. There are symptoms, however unwelcome they may be, that stem from the coincidental intervention of behaviours and events. These symptoms are not, therefore, the consequence of calculated strategic behaviour but more the coincidental result of a range of forces. But it does appear clear that strategic behaviour frequently occurs and has a noticeable impact.

A well-known definition of strategic behaviour is: a 'propensity to shirk, to be opportunistic, to maximise his or her self-interest, to act with guile and to behave in ways that constitute a moral hazard' (Donaldson, 1990; Williamson, 1985). And also: strategic behaviour is 'based on the assumption of rational behaviour – not just of intelligent behaviour, but of behaviour motivated by a conscious calculation of advantages' (Schelling, 1960).

The following characteristics of strategic behaviour can be derived from these quotes:

- Actors behave strategically if the aim of their behaviour is to further their own interest,
- Even if by so doing they damage other interests,
- Because they realise this behaviour could damage their reputation, they camouflage it intentionally.

The three core ideas according to this definition are interest, intent and camouflage (Heuvelhof, 2016).

This book is a journey to discover the strategies that facilitate and enable decision-making in networks. The strategies presented in the preceding chapters enable individual actors, despite their dependencies on other parties, to undertake actions and make decisions through which they can individually bring about their interests and via which they can collectively arrive at decision-making.

So these strategies have two functions: They are needed in order to come to sound collective decision-making, and they serve the interest of individual actors. Think back to the example of the multi-issue game – such a game is attractive for each of the actors individually (they can achieve their interests) and also contains strong incentives to come to collective decision-making. But at some point this balance between the two functions may be disrupted. The interest of the individual actor then takes centre stage, on its own, and the more general interests of the collective decision-making are pushed into the background. That is the moment at which strategy can metamorphose into strategic behaviour – accomplishing the actor's own interest has more priority than serving the interest of collective decision-making. It is, therefore, important to emphasise that there is a distinction between:

- A strategy aimed at achieving individual interest and collective interest, and
- Strategic behaviour whereby the individual interest is more important than the collective interest in coming to decision-making.

A strategy can, therefore, degenerate into strategic behaviour.

Strategic behaviour in networks

Networks are a fertile breeding-ground for strategic behaviour. The web of dependencies in networks makes behaving strategically extremely attractive to actors, especially if there is information asymmetry between the actors and the progress of the decision-making is erratic and nonlinear.

Information asymmetry means that the actors do not possess all the same information (Arrow, 1963; Waterman & Meier, 1998). The reason for this can be quite simple – all the different actors are busy with different issues and are, therefore, interested mainly in information that concerns their own issues. Information related to other issues is of less interest to them. This is why the information actors introduce into processes can often be new, unknown and sometimes disagreeable for other actors. Actors view and evaluate phenomena and processes from the perspective of the information they possess. This phenomenon explains why so much information generated in this sort of process is *contested*.

In this 'fight for the truth' actors can exploit the information asymmetry. They are in the position of being able to decide whether or not to present the information they possess and at what point in time. They also have possibilities to give the information a, for them, favourable '*twist*' – to '*frame*' the information (Bruijn, 2017).

They can keep information hidden; they can allow information to be leaked (Bovens, Geveke, & Vries, 1993); they can write press releases in a way that favours their own standpoint, etc.

The inconsistency of decision-making processes also offers adroit actors many possibilities for strategic behaviour. In networks decision-making progresses in rounds rather than in a linear fashion. The actor configuration can differ per round as can the problems and solutions on the agenda. Actors can make use of this inconsistency with their strategic behaviour. They can, for example, play the *seize-every-opportunity* game – try to gain support for their standpoint at every opportunity in every round. They can also make use of the round-by-round character of the decision-making by employing the salami tactic – try to slowly but surely (slice by slice) gain support for their standpoint.

Strategies and strategic behaviour

So, a strategy can degenerate into strategic behaviour. We will now explain this in respect of five strategies discussed in preceding chapters.

Strategies for redundancy ...

A sensible way to manage the uncertainties and dynamics in networks is to build up and manage a redundant-relationship network. It is obvious that to be able to tackle problems in situations in which actors are dependent on each other, other actors are always needed. This means entering into and maintaining relationships is always necessary. A redundant network is more than a network of actors on which an actor is dependant at a specific time. Redundancy requires relationships with more actors than are strictly necessary for the solution of a problem. Decision-making in networks progresses erratically, and the problems and solutions on the agenda change constantly, which is why a redundant network is very effective in the longer term. Anyone with such a network can cope better with the constantly changing coalitions of actors needed to deal with successive problems.

... can develop into strategic behaviour

An actor who has successfully built-up a redundant network can be tempted to behave strategically.

Opportunistic switching/being unfaithful to partners

It goes without saying that this actor will opportunistically switch partners and constantly activate other parties in his redundant-relationship network. This is not to say that switching in a relationship network is always wrong. The problems and solutions on the table constantly change and to do justice to 'new' problems and solutions an actor must, up to a point, be able to switch. But there is a line that must not be crossed – an actor who constantly switches partners risks being categorised as unfaithful at some point. The dividing line between pragmatic and opportunistic switching is very thin.

Bypassing

Redundancy can also hide in a 'double relationship' with one actor. In this case an actor has two relationships with the same other actor, for example, one relationship at an operational level, the other at a strategic level. Actors who have such double relationships can exploit them in all sorts of ways. They can, for example, unexpectedly introduce information they learned at one level into a negotiation process at the other level. Or during negotiations at an operational level, they can use the possibility of intervention at the strategic level as a threat. This is true strategic behaviour. It can be very effective, but at the same time it can be perceived as very untrustworthy.

Process agreements ...

Parties that need each other can decide to formulate a number of process agreements, or game rules, regarding the way in which they will arrive at decision-making under the leadership of a process manager. Ideally, process agreements of this sort are neutral in respect to the outcome. That means they only facilitate the decision-making and do not give certain parties or interests more chance in the decision-making than others. In other words, all kinds of content-related outcomes are conceivable and possible, based on the agreed rules.

... can evolve into strategic behaviour

Selective activation of actors, issues and framing

How do process agreements come about? Parties in a network are dependent on each other and need each other if they are to solve certain problems. They become aware of this at some point and may realise that, for the sake of collective decision-making, they must make process agreements. Good process agreements are, therefore, necessary in order to reach a decision with a good content. However, the parties can have very different opinions regarding what constitutes good process agreements. More to the point, they can try to negotiate a set of agreements that is the most favourable – for them. How?

- Actors will emphasise their interpretation of the agenda and possibly try to prevent other issues – issues in respect to which they can only lose – making it onto the agenda.
- Actors will think strategically about which other actors should be invited or should be excluded – which actors they expect will support them and which they expect will oppose them. Or they will want to have a monopoly on certain information or authority, which can make excluding certain actors attractive.

In a nutshell: An initial selection of issues and actors can have a steering effect on who will definitely be sitting at the table and what the power relationships in the process will be.

Biased rules and processes

It could well be that the agreed-upon process favours one of the possible content-related outcomes. This could be either very obvious or less obvious. The most strategic are, naturally, process proposals that at first glance appear neutral in content-related terms but that in practice push a specific content-related solution. An agreement about the order in which issues will be discussed could be a determining factor for the outcome of the discussions, without this being obvious immediately and to everyone. Take the decision-making of three friends who want to go on holiday together but disagree about where they should go (Arrow, 1951). The table shows their preferences.

The table shows that friend 1 prefers destination A to destination B and prefers destination B to destination C. The other two friends have different orders of preference. Although they are friends, they do not agree with each other.

Deciding on a holiday destination on the basis of these preferences is problematic. An orderly process rule could be to compare the destinations in pairs and then, if this doesn't produce an outcome, vote.

Suppose that all three friends consider this a fair procedure and that they decide they will first compare and vote on A and B, after which they will compare the winning destination with C. What happens? Friend 2 prefers B to A, but friends 1 and 3 see it differently and opt for A. A is, therefore, the destination that must be compared with C and a glance at the table shows that destination C wins. So the friends will go to C.

But what if B and C were compared first? B would then win and have to be compared with A. And this comparison would result in A being the destination.

According to the first procedure, the friends will go to C, but according to the second procedure, they will go to A! The conclusion: The order in which decisions are made can have a major influence on the outcome, which makes the order subject to strategic behaviour. In the process agreements parties can try to fix a decision-making order that is best for them.

Multi-issue strategies…

Chapter 3 explained the importance of a multi-issue agenda. In a network there are many actors with differing interests. If there is only one issue on the agenda, it is very likely that no decision will be made. Single-issue decision-making creates an either-or situation – parties are for or against something and have an incentive to formulate their standpoint more and more incisively because there is nothing in it for them to negotiate.

Multi-issue decision-making is far more attractive. The agenda includes a number of attractive issues for each of the actors. This makes participation in

Table 6.1 Three friends and their preferred holiday destination

Friends	Destinations in order of preference
Friend 1	A > B > C
Friend 2	B > C > A
Friend 3	C > A > B

the decision-making process attractive, and there is an incentive to play a give-and-take game. There are incentives for cooperative behaviour because there are changing coalitions per issue. Learning is possible. And, not unimportant, the need to reach a package deal together means an actor who behaves opportunistically or inflates his claims is often corrected by the other actors.

... may develop into strategic behaviour

These multi-issue strategies can also lead to strategic behaviour

A selective multi-issue portfolio

Opting to deal with and decide about several issues at the same time will, in general, work out well, but the precise compilation of the multi-issue portfolio can have a considerable influence on the result of the package deal. By adding certain issues to the agenda and excluding others, you influence the circle of actors participating in the decision-making and with that the power relationships in the process and thus the outcome. These relationships may not be immediately obvious to a relative outsider, but an insider will immediately see the connection between the agenda, the involvement of actors and the outcome of the decision-making. This information edge makes strategic behaviour around the composition of the agenda tempting.

It is also conceivable that a multi-issue agenda is compiled in such a way that one actor's prospects for gain are far greater than another actor's. Chapter 3 indicates that it can be difficult to withdraw from a process. Perhaps an actor realises at the end of a process that he has made less gain than the others – but also that he cannot withdraw from the process so must tolerate the excess gain of the others. Even worse, this actor might also realise that this outcome is inherent to the selected multi-issue agenda – and, therefore, was a given right from the start of the process. It would appear that one of the other actors has behaved strategically.

Horse-trading

Negotiating multiple issues at the same time in a single process can easily lead to horse-trading. Horse-trading means issues that in terms of content are separate from each other are traded for each other. Many actors will be of the opinion that this is wrong when there is no connection between these issues in terms of content. If, for example, two political parties are negotiating with each other and one wants more infrastructure and the other a supple immigration policy, they can trade these issues – the first receives extra infrastructure, the other a more generous immigration policy. Or, another example, one party has lower taxation for top incomes on its agenda, while the other party advocates more supple rules for abortions. The result could be a *deal* in which an ideological theme like abortion is traded for a revised sharing of income.

Strategies for accomplishing negotiated knowledge ...

Chapter 1 introduced the unstructured problem phenomenon. What is applicable for this type of problem is that actors not only disagree about the facts on which a problem analysis is based but also about the norms with which the solution must comply and the balance between these norms. This means that the gathering of facts alone is not enough to arrive at a widely supported solution for these problems. The facts must not only be gathered, they must also be negotiated – as must the norms with which the solutions must comply and the solution itself. 'Knowledge' is not enough to bring this sort of problem to a solution, *negotiated knowledge* (Jasanoff, 2009) is needed. An actor who wants to achieve negotiated knowledge in a network must introduce strategies to accomplish this.

These strategies are, on the one hand, necessary to arrive at a good and supported picture of the problems and possible directions in which solutions must be sought. On the other hand, they also offer entry points for strategic behaviour. The actors who can play out their information edge have particularly good possibilities for strategic behaviour. During the negotiations about the facts, actors will be asked to bring in their knowledge. Thanks to this information asymmetry and their monopoly on certain information, they have an arsenal of possibilities to serve only their own interest without the other actors being able to figure out what they are doing.

... may develop into strategic behaviour

Which strategic behaviours are at actors' disposal during this information negotiation process?

Withholding disagreeable information

The first possibility for strategic behaviour arises at the moment information is brought in. Actors who have the monopoly on information can, in most cases, decide for themselves which information they will share and which information they will withhold. They can withhold information they think will weaken their position in the process. This is particularly the case if other actors have a considerable information deficit and do not know what information is available. This type of behaviour can be built on in many ways.

Dispensing information in small doses to disturb a process

Strategic behaviour can mean that an actor with an information edge who has withheld information early in the process decides to share it at a time that suits him later in the process. This sort of 'new' information can easily have a disruptive effect on the negotiation processes and can lead to considerable confusion, irritation and loss of time – which can serve the actor's purpose. A variation of this behaviour is that this actor feeds this information to a third party, such as the media or a scientific institute, so this third party can then release the information to the public and thus disrupt the process.

Scope optimisation

A second series of possibilities for strategic behaviour arises during the analysis of the available information. Suppose that actors are discussing the effects of a possible new activity, such as a construction project, a new technology or a new medication. One essential decision that must be made, and which will be negotiated, is the scope of this activity. Where will the boundary for charting the effects be drawn? This scope is often geographic in nature: From where will information about the effects be gathered? The scope also has a temporal dimension: Until how far in the future will the effects of the new activity be investigated? A third question related to the scope concerns the demarcation of the reach of the effects to be described. Take, for example, an attempt to analyse the environmental effects of certain activities or products. A boundary to the investigation and charting of the effects must always be drawn for this type of analysis. If you compare the environmental effects of an electric car and a conventional car, you will determine that the CO_2 emissions of the electric car are lower than those of a conventional car. But the scope of this comparison is very limited. An expansion of the scope could mean that the origin of the electricity is included in the analysis. Cars that run on electricity generated in a coal-fired power plant could then come out worse in the comparison. In a nutshell, analysis results can change colour if the analysis system boundaries are changed (Guinée, 2002).

One can imagine the strategic behaviour this can lead to. The choice of a scope is a strategic choice, and actors with an information edge and a good overview are in a position to select a scope that ensures their standpoint will come out of the analysis well.

Passing on risks

In scope discussions the actor with the information edge has many options for playing with possible uncertainties and risks. Take a consortium of companies that has been told by an authority that, although it is interested in a project, the estimated price is too high. The consortium knows that a lower price could make a major contribution towards persuading the wavering client. The consortium can reduce the price by shifting a number of risks it had assumed on its own account in the project proposal over to the client. These risks could include the costs that could arise due to increased inflation during construction. Or the costs related to cleaning up any soil contamination caused by the construction. Thanks to this operation the price tag will look much friendlier, but the final bill could be far higher. The consortium will be aware of this; the client won't always be.

All these instances give the actor with an information edge a wealth of possibilities for intervening in the discussions leading to negotiated knowledge in a way that serves his own interest but that is hidden from the other actors for a shorter or longer period.

Strategies aimed at winners and losers ...

After decision-making it will be apparent that some actors are better off as a result of the decisions, while others are relative or absolute losers. Sometimes actors are aware of gain, or loss, from the moment the package deal is agreed to. At other times this awareness comes much later, when all the consequences of the decisions become clear. And, to make it even more complex, we're not talking about an objective gain/loss account, we're talking about the actors' perception of gain and loss. In any event: After the decision-making winners and losers can feel incentives to behave differently than was agreed upon at the time of the decision. These incentives can easily be turned into actions that deviate from the decision made earlier.

Winners will, in general, be satisfied with the decisions and will continue to support them. However, they could feel an incentive to distance themselves from further cooperation with the other actors as soon as the gain has been received. After all, 'the money is in the bank', so why should they continue cooperating with the other actors?

Losers can be resentful from the beginning and can try to reverse the decision, or at the least circumvent or even sabotage its implementation. In Chapter 2 a number of strategies that could help the losers achieve this were described. These strategies, too, can degenerate into strategic behaviour.

And then there are further strategies to counteract and mitigate these effects – again see Chapter 2.

... can lead to strategic behaviour

This managing of winners and losers can easily take the form of strategic behaviour.

Reframing or distorting effects

As has been said, there is no objective answer to the question of whether a gain or loss has been made – it all comes down to perception. Perceptions can be influenced via *framing*. Framing is a strategy whereby intelligent imagery is used in an endeavour to create a specific picture of reality. When an actor believes he is in a win-lose situation – he wins, the other loses – the actor can try to frame the situation in such a way that the other perceives it as a win-win situation. Or in such a way that although this actor understands it's a win-lose situation, third parties get the impression it's a win-win situation.

Framing can also contribute towards actors who are aware they are losers still remaining committed to the decision because they see that, due to the framing, third parties do not see them as losers. Such a framing can be a sign of respect for the loser. The loss is not made visible to third parties, which limits the loser's loss of face. On the other hand, the line between respectful framing and distorting and embellishing the expected effects of a decision is very fine. Deliberately distorting the expected effects is straightforward strategic behaviour.

Playing with time: prospects of gain

Another strategy for managing losers is to offer them a prospect of gain, for example, by offering them a chance of winning in another decision-making process. Or maybe the decision still includes scope for choices during the implementation through which the losers still have a prospect of gain. Because a future with good prospects is sketched out, the expectation is that the losers will behave more cooperatively in the present. Discipline in the present is 'bought' with the offer of future gain. This can easily result in strategic behaviour if too often these prospects of gain do not materialise and the winners are also aware of this. Support in the present is sought by promising future gain, but as soon as this support is no longer needed, the promise of future gain is withdrawn or not fulfilled.

Follow the power

Losers can be offered the prospect of future gain, but they can also be compensated in the present. An environmental movement that was the loser in the decision-making related to a large infrastructure project can be compensated with green projects elsewhere. Compensating losers can contribute towards gaining their support for a decision (such as the construction of a large infrastructure project). But inevitably the question of how far the compensation should go and which losers should be offered the possibility of compensation will arise. The obvious, but also somewhat cynical, approach would be one in which it is primarily the losers with power – the power to frustrate the implementation of the decision – who can look forward to generous compensation, while other losers must be satisfied with far less. In an extreme case the compensation would be directly proportional to the loser's level of power. Such compensation is unlikely to be widely endorsed. On the other hand, it could be functional for upholding the decision. This would be strategic behaviour.

A summary of strategic behaviour

The strategies described in the preceding chapters contribute towards decision-making in networks. However, the strategies can devolve into strategic behaviour. The five strategies discussed are summarised again below along with examples of the strategic behaviours to which they could easily lead.

Table 6.2 Strategies and strategic behaviours

Strategies	Strategic behaviours
Redundant relationships	• Opportunistic switching/ unfaithfulness • Bypassing
Negotiated rules	• Selective activation of actors, issues and frames • Biased rules and processes
Multi-issue approach	• Selective multi-issue portfolio • Horse trading
Negotiated knowledge	• Disagreeable information is withheld • Information is dispensed in small doses • Scope optimisation • Risks are shifted
Managing winners and losers	• Reframe or distort effects • Play with time • Follow the power/paper over the cracks

What should we think of strategic behaviour?

Putting a nominative value on this type of behaviour is not easy. What is the main normative criticism of strategic behaviour, and how should we value it?

The first point of criticism is that actors' strategic behaviour adversely affects the interests of other players. But this does not, of course, mean that strategic behaviour is normatively deemed bad in every case. It could well be that the actor who behaves strategically serves his own interest with this behaviour and adversely affects (some) other interests but at the same time also serves (some) other interests. The net of the effects for society as a whole could, therefore, be positive, however difficult this is to measure.

A second point of criticism is that strategic behaviour is of itself not acceptable, whatever the eventual consequences. Not only is the sole purpose of strategic behaviour the furthering of one's own interests, but also in many cases, this purpose is camouflaged. It is sneaky and mean behaviour. This normative valuation has another side though. An actor who behaves strategically probably knows how the decision-making game is played. Evidently he is capable of achieving something and bringing movement into a situation that all too easily gets bogged down in the power games of the many other actors. That is a competence that has value, certainly if this actor is fighting for a 'good' cause. Anyone who fights for human rights and can play the game well, which sometimes involves behaving strategically, may be sneaky and mean, but by being this way he is benefitting human rights. That can have considerable social value.

Table 6.3 Strategic behaviour: effectiveness and distribution of gains

	Effectiveness of strategic behaviour: low	*Effectiveness of strategic behaviour: high*
Distribution of the gains from the strategic behaviour: limited		
Distribution of the gains from the strategic behaviour: generous		A mild judgement regarding strategic behaviour

A third point of criticism is that strategic behaviour may have social added value, but does it also pay in the long run? This behaviour may benefit an actor in the short-term, but in the longer term it could damage his reputation and reduce his trustworthiness – and that could jeopardise his effectiveness. Yet even this relationship is not so clear-cut. Trust and strategic behaviour can, to a certain degree, go together. How can it be that these actors who behave strategically are still trusted (Jay, 2010)? Three factors are important in this regard, the expectations in respect of the behaviour of the strategic actor, the effectiveness of his behaviour and the allocation of the gains from his strategic behaviour.

What the expectations are in respect of an actor's behaviour is very important. A solitary use of strategic behaviour will not immediately undermine the trust in this actor if this is the behaviour that was expected from this actor. The actor has done what he was expected to do, and his behaviour did not exceed the boundaries of the expectations.

The second and third factors concern the effectiveness of the strategic behaviour and the allocation of the gains. See the table below.

If the effectiveness is high and the gains from this behaviour are spread around widely and generously, it is likely the other actors will be less negative about the strategic behaviour and that the trust in the actor with the strategic behaviour will not be greatly reduced. The opposite is also possible. How much trust would there be in actors who are not effective and never achieve anything? However well such actors behave, the trust in them will be limited. Something similar applies for actors who are effective but who don't share the gains. This too doesn't engender trust in them. The conclusion: Moderate strategic behaviour and moderate trust can go together. This can be the case if the expectations are not too high and the strategic actor is both effective and willing to share.

This discussion of strategic behaviour makes it clear that allocating a normative value to strategic behaviour is not simple. In the following chapter normative questions related to actors' behaviour will be discussed in more detail.

7   Trust and rules of the games

A paradox

In the previous chapters we took a detailed look at how actors play the game – their individual strategies and the patterns this causes in the decision-making process. Say that an actor is extremely proficient in this game – knows all strategies and also acts strategically. What will this signify for the reliability of this actor? There is a major chance that the others will develop a certain distrust of this party. Those who are always vague about their objectives, who try to turn each topic into a multi-issue game, always want to know everything about others, never set deadlines, link solutions to problems – may lose their reliability.

This results in a dilemma. On the one hand, those who want to have an impact in a network of interdependencies will need to use the strategies described in the previous chapters. On the other hand, those who often or always use these strategies run an important risk: They can lose their reliability or the trust of the other actors. Those who have lost this trust will, of course, not have an impact in a network. This dilemma results in a tricky question: How can an actor play the game and behave strategically without losing the trust of the other actors?

A thought experiment

For a first answer to this question, here's another thought experiment. When someone participates in a decision-making process, together with other actors who are striving for their own interests, is this person allowed to lie?

There are two intuitive answers, which are often given to this question – a straightforward 'no' and a straightforward 'yes'.

No, lying is not allowed – as lying is never good. Those who lie are unreliable. Or yes, lying is OK – of course it is part of the game. Lying is a strategy you need. If you would always tell the other the whole truth, you would checkmate yourself in the game, and you'd never get things done.

There are also other answers, in the line of:

- You may not lie, but you don't have to say everything;
- You may not lie, but you may dose out information;
- You may not lie, but you don't have to give information if no questions are asked;
- Sometimes you protect the other party and serve its interests by not informing this party; and
- It's often unclear what the truth is and what isn't – and it's therefore also not clear what lying is.

Why are we doing this thought experiment? Because lying is all about trustworthiness. Lying can be an effective strategy or a form of strategic behaviour, but someone who lies is also unreliable. It's the tension of Figure 7.1 How do we deal with it?

Say someone is the manager of a major research department in a company. Every other year the department makes a plan for the coming years. In this plan the department indicates what they want to research development-wise and how this contributes to better products and services of this company.

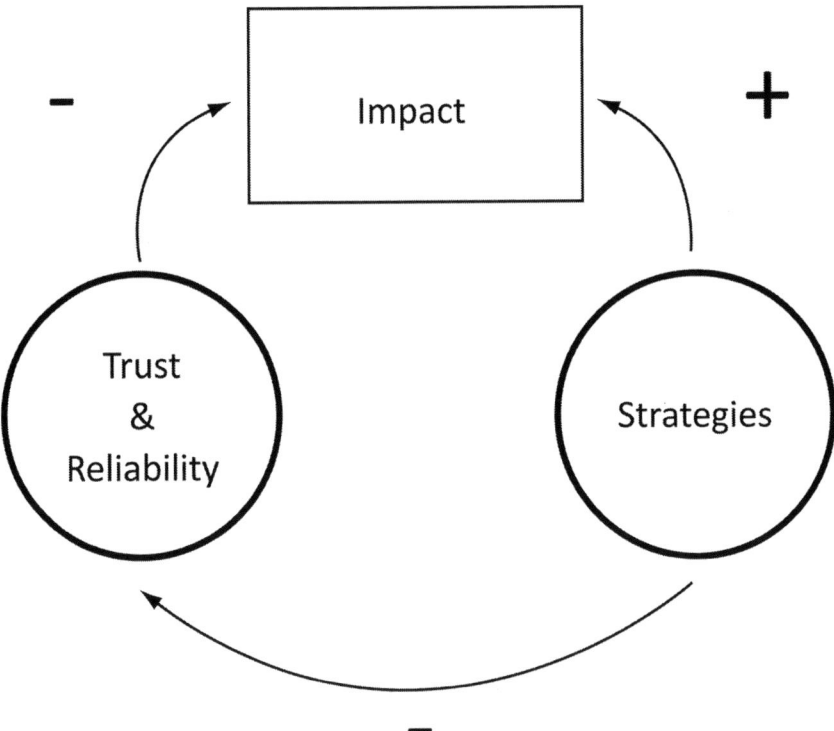

Figure 7.1 The trust-dilemma

The department has developed a plan and the execution of this plan will cost 100 units. The company's manager must talk to the chief financial officer (CFO) to obtain a budget. The manager gives a presentation with an overview of the plans and then asks for 120. This is followed by a negotiation – and eventually a budget of 98 is assigned by the CFO.

One of the employees of the research department subsequently sees the CFO at a reception. They start talking, and the employee tells the CFO that the plan that was made at the time would cost 100. The CFO now knows that the estimated costs were 100 and that the manager asked for 120.

Which conclusion will the CFO draw from this? That the manager is completely unreliable? Probably not. The conclusion will probably be as it so often goes: Managers suggest plans for the CFO and ask for more than they need. This is simply how the game of decision-making works. If we formulate it very sharply: The manager lied, but this does not lead to the CFO believing that the manager is unreliable.

Now this thought experiment undergoes a small change. The research department comes to the conclusion that a budget of 100 is needed; the manager negotiates with the CFO and asks for a budget of 180. Eventually the negotiation results in a budget that is considerably lower than the requested 180.

Once again one of the employees of the research department meets the CFO, who finds out that 100 was needed and 180 was asked. Will the CFO find the manager unreliable now? Probably. In both situations the manager behaved strategically and lied. In the first case this doesn't lead to the conclusion that the manager is unreliable; in the second case it does. Why? Someone who needs 100 and asks for 120, inflates a claim, but does this proportionately. Someone who asks 180 when 100 is needed, is also asking too much but not proportionately.

Apparently, there is a rule of play never mentioned on paper but tacit in the decision-making game: You may inflate a claim, but you must do this proportionately. No organisation has a manual that says that you may ask twenty percent more than you need in negotiations with the CFO. It's a rule that will arise in networks of repetitive interdependencies. If an actor continuously inflates his or her claims to unreasonable proportions, there will come a time when there is a loss of trust in this actor among the other parties. Those who stick to the rule of play of proportionality will be regarded as reliable – those who don't, as unreliable.

Say that the manager of the research department finds lying or inflated claims entirely unacceptable. The claim for the CFO will then be 100, and there is a good chance that the manager eventually gets 80.

Of course this manager has a point: Lying is wrong. Those who constantly lie in their relations are acting immorally. Yet it is important here to distinguish professional and personal trustworthiness. Behaviour that counts as reliable in professional relations isn't always so in personal relations. Those who lie in professional relations or tell the truth when it suits them can be reliable as long as they take account of the rule of play of proportionality. Those with similar ideas about truth and lying in a personal, affective relationship will soon be known as unreliable. In a network of interdependencies the relations are, however, professional, and not affective.

Moreover, when parties are in a network, they need to behave strategically if they want to function successfully. There are conflicting interests and, in spite of this, the parties are interdependent: They need each other for the realisation of their own interest. A ban on lying would shut the door on the functioning of the parties in a network. This is often different in personal relations. These are generally minor conflicts of interest, and the relation is entered into voluntarily.

The final step in this thought experiment: Say the manager is so sick and tired of inflating claims that he suggests changing the culture in the organisation. Political game-playing must be stopped, and managers agree that they will no longer lie to the CFO. Everyone speaks the truth and nothing but the truth. This saves a lot of time – all this negotiating is no longer necessary, and this also benefits the organisation's ethical hygiene.

Will it work? Probably not. If everyone only speaks the truth, decision-making loses its flexibility. The manager demands 100, the CFO offers 80, and none of them can be flexible. If there is ambiguity about the truth – 120 is possible but so is 100 – there isn't one truth; there is room for interaction.

Furthermore, there is an important mechanism the parties will be aware of. If all actors in a network have the collective arrangement that lying is not allowed, it could be tempting for an actor to start lying again. To formulate it differently: There is a strong stimulus for actors to then withdraw from the collective arrangement. There is a great reward for this behaviour, in particular for the first actor who no longer adheres to this arrangement. While everyone is prohibited from lying, this actor can seriously expand his space by lying because everyone will still think that the actor is telling the truth.

This can be compared to the well-known game theory situation, the diner's dilemma. Twenty people go out to dinner and have agreed beforehand to evenly split the check. When the group arrives at the restaurant, it turns out that there are only two options: a menu costing 10 units and a menu costing 20. Some people have a low income and suggest that everyone orders a menu of 10. If everyone sticks to this arrangement, each person can be certain that his costs for the dinner are limited to 10. However, because of this arrangement, there is a stimulus to order a menu of 20, particularly by the person who gives his order last. The price per person is then $(19 \times 10) + (1 \times 20)/20 = 10.50$. This means that the only person ordering a menu of 20 just has to pay 0.50 extra.

Others will also do this at a second dinner, for instance, five of the twenty participants. They then pay 2.50 extra for a menu that is worth 10 more. When a third dinner is announced, everyone will think that he or she will get a menu worth more than 10 by paying a small amount extra. If everyone chooses this, everyone will eventually order a menu of 20. Say that in this third dinner five people stick to the old arrangement and order a menu of 10. They then pay 7.50 more than their menu is worth. They face a choice at the fourth

Table 7.1 The diner's dilemma

Number of people choosing a menu of 10	Number of people choosing a menu of 20	Additional costs for a dinner of 20
19	1	0.50
18	2	1
17	3	1.50
16	4	2
15	5	2.50
10	10	5
5	10	7.50

dinner, the outcome of which can be guessed: again paying 7.50 more than their menu is worth or ordering a menu worth twice as much for 2.50 extra.

The mechanism here, therefore, is that the reward for being the first to ignore the collective arrangement is very high. When the parties realise this, they will also be motivated to ignore the collective arrangement. Eventually the agreement will perish because the costs of respecting this arrangement are much too high.

Now the first person to order a menu of 20 has a problem: His behaviour is visible to everyone, and thus due to it, he can lose the trust of others. This is different in negotiations. When someone claims 100 in a negotiation, is this in accordance with the collective arrangement not to make an exaggerated claim? Or has an exaggerated claim been made? This is much less visible then when ordering dinner. This means that perceptions of this behaviour will play a major role for other people, and these perceptions can be fed by many things other than by the behaviour of the person claiming 100.

The thought experiments thus leads to five conclusions:

- In networks, actors will apply strategies to realise their interests, but those who do this without any reserve could be seen as unreliable – because of this it becomes a lot harder for everyone to realise their own interests.
- This is why actors should also adhere to rules of play, which are often implicit and will temper the behaviour of other actors.
- Those who do not adhere to the rules of play get the 'sanction' that other actors regard him or her as unreliable and therefore no longer want to collaborate with this actor.
- There is a distinction between professional and personal trustworthiness – trustworthiness in a network of interdependent relations is not the same as trustworthiness in affective relations.
- Arrangements to withdraw from strategic behaviour have little chance as they are a stimulus for actors to behave strategically again.

In this chapter we search for rules of the game that apply in networks. We distinguish two types of rules:

- Rules related to the decision-making process
- Rules related to the position of actors in decision-making.

Rules of the game related to the position of actors in decision-making

Rule 1: Don't dance on a dead man's grave – the loser deserves respect

A first rule of play concerns the position of the losing actors. Decision-making in networks ideally has the characteristics of a win-win game but can of course also result in an outcome that means gain for one and loss for the other.

Now this rule of play says that the loser needs to be treated with respect. The reason for this is that the other actors will meet the loser in the next round of the decision-making process. If people danced on his grave in the previous round – if the loser was treated disrespectfully – then this could lead to revanchist behaviour. Furthermore, during negotiations it's easier for actors to accept their loss, knowing that no one will dance on their grave. There are two variants of this rule of play:

- *Don't flaunt the booty, enjoy the victory in silence.* The first means that a winner doesn't publically extend his victory as this will focus more attention on the loser and could be a stimulus for revenge. The rule of play is that victory must be enjoyed silently. In public, this means putting victory into perspective and presenting the package deal as a balanced package.
- *The loser acquires the right.* A loser not only deserves respect but also acquires rights. Those who lost out in decision-making process A therefore probably enabled the package deal to happen. They have a right to compensation in decision-making process B.

There are plenty of examples of these rules of play, which are also called a ban on revenge in international politics (Krummenacher, 1985). The winners of World War II made a lot of effort to get Germany back on its feet economically and politically. After World War I, by contrast, the guilt was unilaterally placed on the Germans in a 'War Guilt Act', and major reparations were enforced against Germany . The lesson learned from this is that this seriously interferes with the further collaboration with the loser: The treatment of the loser of World War I was the seed for World War II. After the fall of the Berlin Wall, American president George H.W. Bush was invited to visit Berlin and celebrate the victory over communism. He refused, however, 'to dance on the Wall', because this would be a provocation of the Soviet Union and could trigger a military reaction (Bush & Scowcroft, 1998, p.149).

Rule 2: Do not affect the core values of other actors

Each actor has core values: values that affect the core of his right to exist. These can be professional core values but may also concern the values of someone personally. A major rule of play is that parties in a network may not affect the core values of the other parties. After all, those who affect the core values of an actor, affect the raison d'être of this actor. If this rule of play is violated, the trust between parties can be seriously harmed. An actor whose core values are affected may not be willing to collaborate again. In addition, an actor can see a legitimation of similar behaviour in this, which will impede collaboration for a longer period.

Jonathan Pollard was sentenced to jail in the United States for selling extremely confidential data on the infrastructure of the American secret services to Israel. In 1993 the Palestinian leader Yasser Arafat and Israeli Prime Minister Benjamin Netanyahu, led by US President Bill Clinton, reached an agreement on a large number of Palestinian-Israeli issues. The agreement was concluded, and the ceremony at the White House was planned when Netanyahu threatened to drop the agreement. He laid down an extra condition: the release of Jonathan Pollard, whom he wanted to take to Jerusalem like a kind of trophy (Albright, 2003, pp.324–326, pp.324–326). It's a strategy of linking: link one's own issue (Pollard) to something that has a major chance of being realised (the agreement).

For Madeleine Albright, the American secretary of state, Netanyahu's request was unacceptable. Pollard had been sentenced to life imprisonment by an American judge after pleading guilty to a conspiracy charge. Releasing a convict as part of a political deal is extremely problematic under the rule of law. It suggests that a crime is acceptable if someone has the right friends (Albright, 2003, p.319). With his proposal the Israeli prime minister went against one of core values of a constitutional state – and, therefore, of his American negotiation partners. Madeleine Albright is not very explicit about this in her memoires, but she and Netanyahu never became friends. She calls him 'both disarming and a little insincere'. 'We thought we had an agreement, while this wasn't his intention at all' (Albright, 2003, p.306).

A core value of companies is the confidentiality of company data. An authority that negotiates with companies on environmental measures and wants to view price calculations in order to find out whether the environmental policy is increasing costs, affects the core values of a company. Price calculations are often extremely confidential and important for the competitive position of a company.

If someone's core values are affected, his functioning is almost prohibited. Netanyahu's attempt to get Pollard to Jerusalem can be regarded as harming the core values of the USA. The United States is a democratic constitutional state with an independent judiciary. It wasn't a party in the negotiations between Palestinians and Israelis but acted as mediator. When a mediator is asked to set aside the rules of their own constitutional state for the benefit of a political agreement, the impossible is requested. An American president who has to release an admitted spy as part of a political deal can lose his or her authority.

Those who violate the rule of play of respect for core values make the functioning of others impossible. Core values are non-negotiable. This is why an actor whose vital interests (i.e., core values) are being affected by, for example, a decision regarding interstate traffic will be excused from the rule of play of proportionality: The actor has the right to react disproportionately (Krummenacher, 1985).

Rule 3: Actors must be able to legitimatise the content of the outcome of the process

In Chapters 3 and 4 it was made clear that one of the essences of decision-making in networks consists of linking problems and solutions. This eventually results in a package deal: a package of solutions that results in gain instead of loss for each of the actors involved.

The package will mainly be a reflection of the power relations in the network: Strong parties can probably realise more than weaker parties. In addition, the package is the result of the interaction process. Issues are linked in this process, not because they belong together content-wise, but because the link is a way to get support for the package deal.

In Chapter 4 the distinction was made between the frontstage and backstage of decision-making. Backstage, the process of consultation and negotiation takes place, and the strategies discussed in Chapters 2, 3, 4 and 5 are adopted. Frontstage, the result is communicated and a different language is used, that of the project approach, in which decision-making is a linear and phase-based process. This distinction comes back here because it also results in a normative duty. Here we also give an example of the use of backstage and frontstage.

Take three parties that are negotiating about the construction of several waste incineration plants. They can't agree, so they broaden the agenda: not only the waste incineration plants are to be discussed but also a more stringent admission policy for refugees and the expansion of subsidy facilities for innovative businesses. Thanks to this multi-issue agenda, a package deal is agreed on, in which arrangements for each of these subjects are made.

Each of these parties must be able to present the result to,for instance, their own supporters, the media or their own organisations. Let's suppose that one of the parties was against the construction of the waste incineration plants (due to the environmental burden), but the decision was made to construct them anyway. The party in question can legitimise this result in two ways:

- *Procedural*: The decision is the result of the negotiations. The waste incineration plants will be built, but in exchange another wish of this party – a broader admission policy for refugees – will be honoured.
- *Content-wise*: The waste incineration plants will be built, but several measures have been taken to limit the environmental burden. In addition,

a number of measures have been taken to make maximum use of innovations that promote maximum sustainability of incinerating waste. If these innovations turn out to work, they will also be applied to existing waste incineration plants.

The first justification conjures up the image of horse-trading. The parties have exchanged issues. This can create the perception of opportunism: If other items had been placed on the agenda, the exchange would have been different. This will be especially hard to explain to the losers (for instance, residents who are bothered by the waste incineration plants). If the agenda had 'coincidentally' been different, the result could have also been that the waste incineration plants would not be built.

The second justification is a lot easier to defend. A connection has been made between innovation and the waste incineration plants, which can be easily defended content-wise. The process has apparently not been characterised by horse-trading but by an attempt of the parties to – given the different insights – obtain content-based *enrichment*. The connection resulted in a solution that is more attractive to all parties. The party that was in favour of the waste incineration plants has obtained the installations and can hardly object to the fact that these must be as innovative as possible and will therefore be designed as environmentally friendly as possible. The party opposing the installations now has the chance to improve the environmental performance of existing waste incineration plants. There will also be losers here, but this conclusion is easier to explain.

The rule of play is that each actor in the process must get the chance to explain the content of the process's result. Actors forced by others into a situation where they can only justify the result procedurally, as the result of horse-trading, have a good chance of losing their authority. Everything is apparently negotiable, and an issue can simply be exchanged for a completely different issue. This invokes the image of opportunism and of an unattractive and unreliable actor.

This rule of play has a moderating effect: The parties know during the process that they must be able to explain the outcomes of the process content-wise. This can be a reason for them to renounce certain links (for instance between waste incineration plants and immigration policy).

Rule 4: *A powerful actor should not use its power*

One of the essential characteristics of a network is interdependency: Actors need each other's support and collaboration. Each actor in a network has means of exercising power, but these can be unfairly divided.

- In the interstate network the national states have many interdependent relations. There is no hierarchy. Still the United States appears as the most powerful country on earth: With regard to both military and economic aspects, the United States has the most means.

- In a professional organisation like a hospital there is no hierarchy. The professionals are mutually dependent, as well as dependent on the executive board, while the executive board strongly depends on the collaboration of professionals. Still the executive board generally has the most power: It has the finances and the authorisation to appoint and dismiss.

A major standard in networks is that the powerful actor uses his power – i.e., his ability to influence behaviour– restrainedly. This is called the power paradox (Rosenthal, 1980). There are several reasons for this restraint.

The powerful actor can no longer fulfil his system responsibility

Restraint is necessary because the most powerful actor in a network has system responsibility. The parties in the network depend on each other and will, in spite of conflicting interests, have to cooperate. If the relations between the actors in a network become seriously disrupted, this can have far-reaching consequences: Problems can no longer be solved, dysfunctional conflicts arise between parties, parties feel they are no longer bound by rules of play, etc.

If the relations in a network become seriously disrupted, the most powerful actor becomes indispensable in preventing the consequences and in normalising the relations in the network. We call this the *system responsibility* of the most powerful actor. As the most powerful actor in the interstate network, the federal government has system responsibility: When major adversity occurs in the world, Washington is expected to play a leading role. Only it has the means to face up to this adversity.

Such actors, however, cannot also continually exploit their position of power, as they could lose their authority in the network and thus no longer be able to fulfil their system responsibility. Focussing on the US: if the United States were to intervene in every local military conflict, this could harm its position of power and authority. This hinders US interventions when a worldwide military conflict is impending.

Something similar applies to the manager of a professional organisation – the hospital, for example. A manager has the position of power to solve many problems in an organisation. Managers who are too hands-on and use their position of power too much can at some point lose their authority. They have caused too many minor or major conflicts, have committed too much to certain decisions – which have sometimes led to unwanted outcomes – and have probably also lost their magic. They have become too much of a manager. If a major problem then occurs or the organisation faces important strategic choices, there is a risk that there is insufficient trust in the manager. As a result the manager cannot fulfil his system responsibility.

Loss of the mysticism of power

Restraint is also necessary because the position of power of an actor can erode when the actor uses his means of exercising power. A powerful actor who shows or uses his power invokes unrestrained resistance from other actors, a 'catch as catch can' attitude. A well-known mechanism in this regard is that a powerful actor exerts his power, after which the other actors conclude that the position of power of this actor was weaker than originally thought. The powerful actor has thus lost some of his mysticism. Power is often power because and insofar as it is not used and is not too visible.

To give you an example, we will go back in time to the Roman Empire. When Gaius Julius Caesar Octavianus – the later Emperor Augustus – gained power over what would become the Roman Empire, he no longer had any rivals, making him the absolute ruler over an undivided territory. His adoptive father, Julius Caesar, had been murdered because he presented himself visibly and all too clearly as the most powerful man in the Roman Republic, which resulted in the resistance of others. Augustus did not create the image of an almighty ruler. 'From this moment I had more influence than anyone else, but I didn't have more power than others who were my colleagues in various positions' (Hekster, 2005, p.8). Augustus's power was kept hidden behind the façade of the traditional Roman governance structure. Augustus could remain powerful by not seeming powerful (Hekster, 2005).

The power paradox can also manifest itself in a chief executive officer who constantly carries out one-sided interventions in his company. If this fails several times, his position of power will be strongly reduced, and there will be less of a chance of a future intervention being effective. Two consecutive managers of the Dutch technology company Philips had to experience this. They were brought in as decisive leaders, wanted to impose a complete change on Philips from above and carried out one intervention after another – so-called 'presidential projects'. A number of these projects failed, which caused their authority to decrease. This led to the following complaint of a stock market analyst: 'Every butcher they hire turns into a masseuse' (Business Week, 1999, p.21). Restraint when exercising power is often more sensible. Threatening others with power is often more effective than using the means of power.

Exercising power affects long-term relations

Restraint is finally also important because the powerful actor cannot achieve long-term results in a network without the support of the other actors. While less powerful actors may not be capable of influencing other actors, they do have the power to block decision-making on the initiatives of other actors without anything positive to replace them. If the powerful actor used all of his means of exercising power, the chances of future collaboration with less powerful actors could be wasted.

'Power revealed is power reduced; power concealed is power enhanced', is how Samuel Huntington summarises this paradox. 'Effective power is unnoticed power; power observed is power devalued' (Huntington, 1981, p.75–76).

Rule 5: Consultation and interaction should never be refused

An important rule of play in networks is that actors should never refuse each other the possibility of consultation. This rule of play is especially important when one of the parties has a major chance of loss. Even if it is extremely clear to the parties that the loss to the party in question cannot be avoided, the rule of play that consultation may not be refused applies.

The other actors will reencounter the loser. The losing actor, therefore, must be offered the option to avert his loss until the last moment. If this doesn't happen, then the thought can be created in the loser that his loss could have been prevented and is, therefore, the result of the refusal of others to consult with him. This perception, of course, is not beneficial to the next interaction between the loser and the other parties. The winners will, therefore, prevent the loser from thinking that they are responsible for his loss.

Violation of this rule of play can weaken the position of the winners. The coalition of parties that have agreed to a package deal, as indicated in Chapter 3, always runs the risk that certain parties leave the coalition, thus threatening its collective gain. Those who will potentially disengage can be very sensitive to events that legitimate their resignation. If it turns out that there was no consultation with the loser, who then doesn't participate in the package deal, this can be an important legitimisation to leave the decision-making process (Brands, 2004).

We will again take an example of international politics. After Iraq's invasion of Kuwait, American president George H.W. Bush organised an international coalition against the Iraqis. This coalition also included a number of Arab countries that joined reluctantly.

During this period, Iraq repeatedly stated that it was prepared for further consultation. It was clear to the allies that this consultation would come to nothing. Bush kept imparting, however, that he was willing 'to go the extra mile with Saddam' (Bush & Scowcroft, 1998). After all, a Bush refusal to negotiate could weaken his position in case of an attack. The Iraqis could have stated that Bush did not give them the opportunity to prevent war. This could have broken up the coalition that the Americans needed in order to legitimise their actions: since, in that case, the loser would not have been given the opportunity to stave off its loss.

If this rule of play is violated, however, this gives doubters an attractive opportunity to leave the coalition. They have a procedural argument to end the collaboration. Content-wise, the statement could be that the doubters have no qualms with the package deal, but they cannot agree to it on procedural grounds.

A final reason for this rule of play is that interaction is the central characteristic of processes in networks. Decisions and changes are the result of consultation between the parties in the network. Without interaction nothing is possible in a network, so refusing consultation affects a central feature of a network. Here, too, a reference to interstate traffic can also be interesting. In his study into rules of play in interstate traffic, Heinz Krummenacher formulates the '*Prinzip der Kontaktnahme, -erhaltung und des Nichtausschlagens von Verhandlungangeboten*' (Krummenacher, 1985, p.124). The interaction between states should continue, also in a serious conflict. If formal consultation is refused, there is often still informal consultation. If political consultation is refused, there is often official consultation or trade relations are used for consultation.

Rule 6: Respect the principle of reciprocity: one good turn deserves another

Decision-making in a network, in which parties depend on each other, is only possible when the principle of reciprocity is adopted: Duties are reversible. Actor A owes actor B something in the knowledge that actor B will owe actor A something the next time. Actors can make concession in negotiations or help others in solving their problems, which according to the rule of play of reciprocity means that they offer social credit. At other moments – in other negotiations or if they have a problem and others a solution – they can recoup the credit from these actors. In cultural anthropological research this principle is known as giving gifts. Those who give a gift acquire a right: 'a gift is received with a burden attached' (Mauss, 1990, p.41).

An example of violating this rule is when a party seriously exaggerates its own loss.. This leads to a lot of compensation *by* others but without providing a lot of compensation *for* others. A variant to this is when a party takes on such an extreme position from the beginning of the negotiations that it makes it seem as if a lot is being given so a lot needs to be compensated.

If a party doesn't respect this rule of play, it will be at the expense of his trustworthiness. Other parties will approach this party with distrust because they aren't sure that a possible loss on their part will be compensated or that overcompensation will always be demanded by exaggerating loss.

Rule 7: Act proportionately, normatively speaking

The rule of play of proportionality was already discussed in the thought experiment. Withholding, exaggerating, dosing out or providing information when the *policy window* is open: It's all allowed, as long as it's proportionate.

This rule of play of proportionality also applies to the other strategies. Some examples:

• Proportionality is a rule of play when connecting issues: Some issues are so unequal that linking them is not proportionate. Those with a practical problem should not link it to an institutional issue – which applies for a longer period and determines the traffic between actors – as the consequence can be that institutions are subsequently influenced by an operational issue that just so happened to occur at the moment that the institutional issue needed to be decided upon.

- Compensating losers must be proportionate: A party that accepts its loss in the hope of receiving a lot of compensation for this violates the rule of proportionality.
- Threatening is allowed in a network: It can make the other party more receptive to the wishes of the threatening party. Threatening proportionately means that a relatively unimportant proposal is threatened with severe consequences if a party doesn't agree to the proposal.

Proportionality can also have a strong normative dimension: A connection may be made or a window of opportunity used that is not proportionate normatively. An example: 'Doing a Jo Moore'. Jo Moore was a political advisor to the British government who sent an e-mail message on 11 September after planes had flown into the Twin Towers in New York City but before they collapsed to the spokespeople in her department: 11 September was 'a very good day' to 'get out anything we want to bury' (Committee on Public Administration, 2002). 'A good day to bury bad news' refers to a strategy discussed in Chapter 4: Those who want to achieve support should be alert to windows of opportunity. Decision-making about certain issues has a chance of success if there is a huge amount of attention for other subjects.

Jo Moore's strategy was regarded as an unacceptable form of opportunism. Connecting and disconnecting are allowed and you may use windows of opportunity, but there are moral limits. If an actor is known for using the most dramatic events to serve his own interests, this can affect the trustworthiness of that actor.

The question is, of course, what is still proportionate and with which actions the rule of proportionality is violated. There is only one answer to this question: This is determined by the negotiating parties. Some parties will tolerate more than others; sometimes parties will tolerate more at some times than at others. This rule of play is clear, but it doesn't come into use and is only fleshed out when parties appeal to it in negotiations..

Rules of the game related to the decision-making process

Rule 8: Show respect for the ritual of the process

Decision-making in networks sometimes has a strong ritual character. The rule of play calls for respecting this ritual (Frey, Benz, & Stutzer, 2004). This respect has two aspects:

- Prudence is called for when making short cuts – a short cut entails that someone skips a few steps in a process because this strategically benefits this actor or because the process outcome is already known. The rule is that the process should be gone through, even if it doesn't add up strategically or the result is already known;

- Prudence is called for when making someone else's strategy more explicit by exposing it.

The process should be gone through

We will once again take the example of the research manager and the CFO who negotiate about a budget for a research project. The CFO who is confronted by a claim costing 120 units probably already knows at the time what amount the research manager actually wants to come to. The research manager knows that the CFO knows this. Still they go through the process of interaction: presenting a claim, substantiating it, contesting the substantiation, making a counteroffer, threatening not to finance the project at all, threatening that the company will undergo major harm if the project is not carried out, etc. This entire interaction process has a strong ritual character, especially if both parties know from the start what the outcome of the process will more or less be.

This rule of play states that this ritual should be respected. Actors have to go through this process or ritual. What would happen if one of the parties suggests a 'short cut'? If the CFO suggests from the start of the process to make a budget of 100 available and skip the ritual? To omit strategic behaviour?

This isn't sensible from a strategic perspective. If the CFO doesn't behave strategically, it's more attractive to the research manager to do this, for instance by not regarding the bid of 100 as a final offer but as an opening bid. Those who are too early with the final bid burn their own fingers.

This chapter, however, mainly concerns trustworthiness. Why can a 'short cut', and therefore a lack of respect towards the ritual, be a sign of untrustworthiness?

First and foremost, because this doesn't give the other actors the chance to play the game: list their arguments and give and take. Apparently the presumption is that the actors in this process could present entirely predictable arguments and that the process could also develop entirely predictably. This can be a form of disrespect for the other actors. This certainly applies when the process – more than in the example of the research manager and the CFO – is a multi-issue process. The development of a multi-issue process and its result are by definition unpredictable. Those who don't respect the ritual, don't respect the other actors.

Secondly, a process of interaction leads to a result, mainly in the form of a package deal. It's of major importance that actors can trust each other in the execution of this package deal, as opportunistic behaviour lies in wait otherwise. An actor whose share of the package deal is realised could be tempted to end all further collaboration in the continued execution of the package deal, as his own share has been settled.

Mutual trust can only occur in a process. During the interaction process the parties get to know each other and each other's points of view and interests. They play the game of give and take. Thanks to this process, the result is commonly shared. The actor who takes a short cut doesn't enable the creation of trust and runs the risk that the result is a less common one. The less this is a common result, the stronger the stimuli for opportunism after the profit has been paid out for a specific party. Respect for the ritual, therefore, is beneficial for the creation of trust.

A metaphor that clarifies this rule of play is that of the mourning process. When a dramatic event occurs, someone often goes through a mourning process. There is a phase of numbness, sadness, anger, resignation and acceptance. These phases have a certain predictability. Say that someone is confronted by a dramatic event. It would be useless to show this person that the outcome of the mourning process is set – some form of acceptance – and then advise them to take a short cut skipping the other phases. Someone cannot accept something until all the other phases have been experienced. Acceptance arises during the process. It's no different with processes in a network: The process must be experienced in order for a good result to be achieved, even if the content is already known.

Don't always expose the strategies of the other

The rule of play respecting the ritual has another implication. It can be tempting for a party to make the strategy of the other more explicit or to expose it. Such exposure can be very effective. If an actor tries to design a multi-issue process and another actor makes this explicit, this can result in the strategy failing. Other parties can refuse to mention issues, mention too many issues or, in spite of the multi-issue agenda, not be willing to enter the process. Those who plan a process of connecting and disconnecting and impart that they will no longer join such a process because they see it as horse-trading hinder the decision-making process.

Parties in a network can, however, only achieve successful collaboration if they apply the strategies of the previous chapters. If the result of exposure is that these strategies cannot be sufficiently applied, collaboration cannot come about. Respect for the ritual implies that the strategy of exposure and making agendas more explicit is renounced. While the parties know that a strategy of – for instance – multi-issue decision-making is used, they play the game and do not make the strategy of the other more explicit. Without such respect, there is a risk that there won't be any collaboration.

Rule 9: Don't play chess on two boards at the same time

'Wait-and-see' or 'keep-options-open' strategies can be very attractive to actors. As long as they don't commit to collaboration with certain actors, they have the possibility of seeking collaboration with others that is probably more attractive.

This strategy, however, has a major limitation: the rule of play that one shouldn't play chess on two boards at once. This would entail actor A negotiating about certain issues with actor B while also negotiating about the same issues with actor C without B and C being aware of this.

Why is playing chess on two boards at the same time a form of untrustworthiness? If actors B and C have the perception that they are a unique partner of A, they will adapt their behaviour to reflect this. They can, for instance, provide A with information they would not give out normally. We again use the example of the negotiations between the CFO and the research manager. During the negotiations the research manager can provide the CFO with new information in order to get a good result. He or she can, for instance, indicate that the project can easily be divided and that not all sub-projects are equally important. For the research manager this information is of strategic importance, and he will not reveal it until he thinks that this will increase the chance of a good deal. Say that the CFO plays chess on several boards at once. The CFO negotiates with a university about a budget for the exact same research project. This can be attractive from the CFO's perspective, who now has two offers – one from his own research manager and one from a university — and can choose the best one. The CFO's trustworthiness will, however, strongly suffer from playing chess on two boards at the same time. The research manager invested a lot in a relation with the CFO, released crucial information, probably almost had a deal but heard at the last moment that the deal with the university was better. The research manager probably would have not revealed the information that is crucial to the manager if he had known that the CFO was also active on another chessboard.

In addition, when parties adhere to the rule that one shouldn't play chess on two boards at the same time, they probably also miss opportunities. When the university negotiates with the CFO, a third party – another company for instance – can make the university a more attractive offer during the negotiation process. If the university adheres to the rules of play and has already invested a lot in the relationship with the CFO, it will not go into the offer of this third party, even though it may be more attractive than that of the CFO.

If the CFO turns out be playing chess on two boards at the same time and the negotiations with the university break off, the image may be formed that negotiations with this CFO are always risky: You never know whether he is also speaking to others. You can have the impression that a relationship of trust is formed, but the CFO can still choose another party at the last moment. Naturally, the CFO's trustworthiness will strongly suffer from this.

Playing chess on two boards at the same time is no problem if this was imparted to the other parties in advance. If the research manager and the university know that they are in competition for the research budget, this will not influence the CFO's trustworthiness. An entirely different situation then arises: not a negotiation between the research manager or the university and the CFO but a procurement, which has entirely different rules of play.

Rule 10: During the process a ban on the exit option arises, as well as a decision-making duty

A number of aforementioned rules of play can lead to actors being condemned to endless consultation, which makes decisions impossible. After all, the rules of play limits the strategic manoeuvring space of the actors in a network. Core values of actors may not be affected; the loser has the right to extra negotiations; the loser acquires the right to compensation; and the ritual must be respected, even when the outcome of a process is more or less set. The rules of play can then impede decision-making, especially when one considers that actors can also make strategic use of the rules of play. The loser can continuously ask for extra efforts from other actors or he can strongly exaggerate his loss, so the need for compensation increases. Actors can formulate their ordinary interest as a core value to try to make it unnegotiable. An actor can try to endlessly extend the ritual of decision-making, so decision-making is prevented.

In each network there will be rules of play to prevent this behaviour. The essence of such a rule of play is twofold:

- They impose the duty on the party to, after some period, proceed to decision-making; and
- They prohibit parties from, after some time, using the exit option and leaving the process.

The presence of rules of play means that a party can no longer withdraw from the decision-making process and must commit to a fair completion of this process. The underlying thought is that parties participating in a process invest in each other: They incur expenses (money, time), provide each other with information and restrain their strategic behaviour by adhering to the rules of play. When parties adhere to the rule that chess isn't allowed to be played on two boards at the same time, they probably also lose out on attractive offers from third parties. When parties invest so much in each other, this creates obligations: There could come a time when the parties have invested so much in each other that they are obliged to make a joint decision and agree on a package deal.

This obligation is formalised in many legal systems by the principle of precontractual good faith. Parties that negotiate with each other need to behave reasonably and fairly towards each other. Part of this reasonableness and fairness can be that they are bound by certain negotiation results, even if there isn't an official agreement yet. For instance in 2002, KLM Royal Dutch Airlines was fined 175 million by an international arbitration committee because it unilaterally broke off collaboration a year-and-a-half after the start of negotiations, and following an agreement in principle, on a strategic alliance with the Italian carrier Alitalia.

Rule 11: Respect procedures: no intermediate change of the rules of play

Say that all actors in a network consistently adopt the strategies of the previous chapters. Also say that each actor does this when it suits him. When actors have made a connection between problems and solutions, this can lead to support for a package deal, but there may be other actors who want to disconnect these problems and solutions. Or they connect the concept package to other subjects, which reduces the chance of support. When there is a decision and its execution is under discussion – and for which some room is offered – actors may try to reverse the decision or thwart its execution.

Thomas Hobbes's *Homo homini lupus* would apply to such a situation: One actor is a wolf; win-win decision-making is unlikely. Decision-making becomes a fight of everyone against everyone else. Everyone pushes and shoves in the decision-making process, and no result ever holds out for long. Think of the example of the dancing table. Pushing and shoving can then go on endlessly, even if the table has ended up in a corner.

How can consolidated decision-making come about if they are conflicting interests when it comes to *content*? Actors do this by agreeing on a number of *procedures* they will adopt in the process of consultation and negotiation. After all, procedures provide some predictability for the behaviour of parties and the course of decision-making, thus preventing the process from merely being unsurveyable chaos. The greater the interests in a network, the greater the importance of procedures. Content-wise the parties disagree – so content-based agreements are no longer possible – but by agreeing on several procedures, some order can be brought to the decision-making process (Bruijn, Heuvelhof, & Veld, 2000).

An example is a reorganisation in a company for which there is a lot of resistance. Resistance can lead to chaos, and procedures can help prevent this. The procedure can, for instance, consist of a number of steps:

- First, there is an overall plan that is discussed with the staff and put down in writing after their input;
- Subsequently, the plan is developed in detail in a number of scenarios in which the personnel consequences are described; these scenarios are also discussed with the staff, after which a scenario is chosen;
- After this, the managers are asked whom they are putting forward for dismissal;
- The employees whom they propose to dismiss get the opportunity to lodge an objection with the management;
- After the management has made a decision, the plan becomes final.

Now it can be attractive from the management's perspective, to change this procedure at any moment during the process. For instance, the management unilaterally decides not to develop a number of different scenarios for staff reduction but to present just one proposal. This is an intermediate changing of the procedure or of the rules of play. This can affect the management's trustworthiness. Perhaps a number of managers wanted to use the discussion about the scenarios to safeguard their own interest and to indicate where dismissals are required elsewhere. This chance is now taken away from them. Furthermore, if the management makes a procedure proposal in a future decision-making process, reactions to this will probably be sceptical: What are procedural proposals of actors worth if these actors subsequently change the procedures during the game?

Normative dilemmas

The aforementioned rules of play restrain the behaviour of parties in a network. This feeds mutual trust. In addition, there are some dilemmas of a normative nature, which the parties in a network can be confronted by. We discuss this and indicate that there are two ways of dealing with these dilemmas: prudently or opportunistically.

Selection

Actors in a network face the choice concerning with which actors they want to enter into a coalition. They will in many cases 'selectively activate' a network Scharpf, 1978): There is collaboration with certain actors and not with others. In addition, the issue may arise as to which networks actors are allowed to join and from which are they excluded.

These forms of selection can be based on content-based and strategic criteria. When applying these content-based criteria, actors are examined for expertise concerning an issue or to what extent they have content-based interest in an issue. Strategic criteria concern the issue of power: Which actors have the power to bring a decision-making process to a favourable conclusion?

A problem can arise when these criteria lead to different results. For instance, actors may have their interests brought into the discussion but remain outside the decision-making process because they have insufficient power. The involvement of these actors can further complicate decision-making. Power considerations then overshadow content-based considerations. The dilemma here is whether selection only takes place on the basis of power considerations or whether content-based considerations also play a role.

Threats

Part of the description of strategies in Chapter 5 includes the idea that threats Liu, 2009; Sinaceur, Van Kleef, Neale, Adam, & Haag, 2011) play a major role. Negotiations can become more effective if simultaneous unilateral measures are threatened. Threats have the benefit of potentially generating win-win situations: the gain of actors then consists of preventing a loss.

These similar forms of guidance can be extremely effective, but their legitimacy can be debatable. After all, those who make threats put others under pressure, especially if they are apparently willing to break off consultation and carry out the threat. This can severely harm the relation between these parties – who might need each other in the future.

Threats can therefore be effective, but those who often make threats, risk losing their trustworthiness. Prudence when threatening means that this is an *ultimum remedium*, which should be used reluctantly. Opportunism when threatening means that an actor constantly uses this instrument.

Exchange

One question about the legitimacy of strategic guidance concerns linking problems and solutions, giving guidance the character of exchanging ('linkages').

Its legitimacy can be problematic – think of, for instance, the example where waste processing plants are exchanged for a more stringent immigration policy. The dilemma here is that an actor may be reluctant to link or exchange issues – out of the principle that not everything can be negotiated, exchanged or linked.

Collaboration

Guidance in a network means forming coalitions: Parties jointly form a win-win coalition. Parties are involved in a coalition, but parties are also excluded. Choosing coalition parties is largely related to considerations of power, for instance, the question of whether a party has production or blockage power.

The question now is whether each party is allowed to join a coalition or whether there are moral limits. Many countries have laid down strict rules when it comes to negotiations with organised crime, although a coalition between police and criminals offers many problem-solving possibilities. Inter-state traffic also gives examples of this dilemma. In World War II the Allies turned out not to be capable of dispelling Hitler's fascist regime without forming a coalition with the equally objectionable regime of Stalin: The Devil was dispelled by Beelzebub. Are there major limitations to collaboration with others, or can there always be collaboration with everyone?

Process orientation

What is a good result of a decision-making process in a network? Earlier, in the discussion of evaluation in networks, we listed several evaluation criteria:

- The extent of satisfaction of actors: A process is a success if actors are satisfied about the outcome of the decision-making process.
- The extent to which future collaboration is possible: A process is a success if all parties are willing to continue their collaboration with regard to other issues.

- The extent to which a process was fair: A good process is a process in which parties are treated fairly, even if they aren't entirely satisfied about the result.

These are merely procedural criteria. There is also an important content-based criterion: Did the parties learn during the process? There is a risk that parties in a network limit themselves in the evaluation to procedural criteria: Satisfaction, future collaboration and a fair process are then more important than content-based criteria. Here they can appeal to the unstructured character of problems, which never have one right solution. This can result in parties accepting an incorrect or unfair outcome. Here the choice is between procedural or content-based evaluation criteria.

Opportunistic or prudent treatment of dilemmas

The aforementioned dilemmas are relevant to all actors functioning in networks. Private as well as public actors face these decisions, which have been summarised in the next table.

The table indicates that there is an opportunistic and a prudent way of dealing with these dilemmas. Both ways of dealing with this have consequences for the effectiveness of the action of an actor. After all, the underlying thought when formulating the rules of play in this chapter is that actors repeatedly meet in the middle. If this assumption is right, an actor who continually chooses the opportunistic variant every time will invoke opportunistic behaviour of the other actors in the network, or the actor will lose the trust of the other actors.

In the short term, opportunistic behaviour in networks will often be rewarding. The same applies to opportunistic behaviour in networks with few repetitive interdependencies. An actor who appreciates durable relations, however, will need to take a prudent attitude towards the dilemmas. Those who, in spite of this, choose the opportunistic variant, may be confronted by the loss of legitimacy. The credibility of an actor will be reduced and so will his capability of cooperating with others.

Concluding remarks

To conclude this chapter we will also make some remarks about the rules of play.

The rules of play are utilitarian: Actors will stick to them because they are useful. An actor who has repetitive interdependencies with other actors cannot function in the long run if the actor is continuously dancing on others' graves, affecting core values, changing rules of play intermediately, etc. If interdependencies aren't repetitive, then there is in principle little attraction for an actor to adhere to the rules of play. After all, the rules of play limit the options of strategic use and thus the possibility of realising one's own interest.

Table 7.2 Normative dilemmas

	Methods of dealing: opportunist	Methods of dealing: prudent
Selecting	Selection only on the basis of considerations of power	Selection also on content-based grounds
Threatening	Frequent threats	Restrained threats
Exchanging	Being prepared to exchange everything	Normative limitations to what is suitable for exchange
Forming coalitions	When forming a coalition, frequently letting the end justify the means	Restraint when forming a coalition with Beelzebub
Process orientation	Limited to procedural standards	Procedural and content-based standards
Results	• Short term: effective, 'on scoring points' • Long term: durability of relations is affected • Legitimacy is problematic	• Short term: not 'scoring points' • Long term: beneficial to durability of relations • Promotes legitimacy

Various situations can be conceived in which actors do not adhere to the rules of play. For instance, it is possible that certain actors estimate a situation as hierarchic, while other actors define this as a network. From this perception the rules of play will not apply, from the second perception they will. Parties can be inexperienced. They report to a network for the first time and simply don't know about the use of rules of play. How does insight then come in such situations that rules of play are useful? How can parties learn about useful rules of play? After all, many of the rules of play discussed haven't codified.

Parties can only do this by participating in decision-making processes. When they do, they will learn that dependencies are repetitive, that opportunistic behaviour doesn't pay off and that certain types of behaviour – dancing on a grave, affecting core values, etc. – affect one's own trustworthiness. As the relations between actors become more repetitive, there is a greater chance of these learning processes.

8 Process and content

There are two frequently mentioned objections to the network approach. The first is that when decisions are made in a network the process and the decision-making game are more important than the content. When facts and causalities are social constructions and negotiable, the result canbe, of course, a disinterest in facts and causalities. Everyone construes his own reality, and the policy analyst is dismissed as a *numbers-cruncher* and a *bean counter*.

The second objection follows on from this. When content is very much underplayed, the decision-making game appears to be determined solely by power. It's not the actor who speaks the truth who achieves his goals but rather the actor who has the power sources and the dexterity to play the game well.

Such images can give sustenance to a common misunderstanding regarding networks: Decision-making in networks would be a deviant form of decision-making. The conception is then that phased, project management–based decision-making represents an ideal and that network-based decision-making is a deviation from this ideal. Such a deviation may have to be tolerated temporarily (due to the presence of a strong network structure), but all efforts must be focused on achieving the decision-making ideal. The consequence of this view maybe, for example, that the top echelons of organisations do their utmost to revert the organisation to a hierarchy. With the reincarnation of the hierarchy, the decision-making, so goes the thought, will also once again be 'rational' and therefore better. 'Better' frequently has two meanings: The process is more transparent and predictable – because the decision-making process is phased and sequential – and the content of the decision-making is dominant rather than the game and the process.

Table 8.1 illustrates this reasoning. The judgement of the network approach is negative in such reasoning.

The actions of the parties in a network are dictated by power considerations. They think and act on the basis of their own interest and not on the basis of the general interest. In a power game parties continuously try to maximise their own interests. Content-related arguments are only interesting if and to the extent that they serve a parties own interest. Facts and causalities are constructed in such a way as to fit in with the own interest, or the facts are negotiated with the other parties. Decision-making thus acquires the characteristics of a mafia. It's true that within networks certain game rules apply, but as their sole aim is to support the power game, they only have a utilitarian function. Moreover, the mafia also has strict game rules that are equally utilitarian. Their purpose is to preserve the organisation.

The opposite of this is an approach in which a problem is looked at from a content point of view and in which justice is done to facts and causalities. There is no investment in power games; the investment instead is in careful analyses. These analyses lead to outcomes that can clash with the interests of certain parties – possibly even with the interests of a majority of these parties. A party with integrity will, however, be willing to learn from the analyses. Such a learning process will give a party more than will the constant hawking of its own interests. The adage 'speaking truth to power' is applicable here.

So which picture is correct? The answer depends on several factors, including the type of problems being discussed. As soon as unstructured problems are involved, it becomes impossible to talk about THE problem and THE solution. Multiple definitions of the problem and the solution are possible. If such a problem has to be solved in a network, the different perceptions the parties have of the problem or of its solution are justified. It is then also wrong to talk about a personal interest versus a general interest. Every party in a network has a justified interest.

This means that the images talked about above can change. A 'careful analysis' of an unstructured problem can lead to a problem definition and solution that fits in with the perception of one of the parties. There are, however, other careful analyses possible that lead to other problem definitions and solutions that fit in with the perceptions of other parties. If a party carries out an analysis and then takes the standpoint that this means the problem and the solution are known, this does not do justice to other perceptions and interests. It makes one think of a form of Kremlinology: There is only one fixed definition of the truth that is imposed on others as far as possible. The result is that learning is impossible.

A network approach is based on the concept that every party in a network has his or her own perception of the truth and, therefore, also has justifiable interests. These interests are respected, and every party is entitled to bring his or her interests into the decision-making. In so doing a party may behave strategically, as long as they play by the rules of the game. These game rules are always aimed at cooperation and moderating the strategic behaviour of the parties in the network. A decision that can count on sufficient support from the participating parties is arrived at in a process of negotiation. Decision-making in networks thus approaches the democratic ideal: There is plurality, and a decision is made that reflects the diversity of problem and solution definitions and that is sufficiently widely supported.

The four images given here are, naturally, ideal-typed. Table 8.1 makes it clear that decision-making in a network always involves the risk that it will develop into a pure power-game with mafia characteristics. However, it also makes it clear that thinking of a network-approach as a deviant form of decision-making is wrong.

Table 8.1

	Negative judgment	Positive judgement
Hierarchy and linear decision-making	*Kremlin:* Unilateral decision-making is imposed on other actors.	*Speaking truth to power:* Facts and analyses determine the course of the decision-making process.
Networks and messy decision-making	*Mafia:* Power and interests determine the course of the decision-making process.	*The democratic ideal:* All parties have legitimate interests, and decision-making reflects this plurality.

Bibliography

Albright, M. (2003). *Madam secretary: A memoir*. New York: Miramax.

Andersson, M., & Mol, A. P. (2002). The Netherlands in the UNFCCC process–Leadership between ambition and reality. *International Environmental Agreements: Politics, Law and Economics*, 2(1), 49–68.

Andrews, K. M., & Delahaye, B. L. (2000). Influences on knowledge processes in organizational learning: The psychosocial filter. *Journal of Management Studies*, 37 (6), 797–810.

Arrow, K. (1951). *Social choice and individual values*. Hoboken, NJ: John Wiley & Sons.

Arrow, K. J. (1963). Uncertainty and the welfare economics of medical care. *American Economic Review*, 53(5), 941–973.

Bendor, J. B. (1985). *Parallel systems: Redundancy in government*. Berkeley: University of California Press.

Bó, P. D. (2005). Cooperation under the shadow of the future: experimental evidence from infinitely repeated games. *The American Economic Review*, 95(5), 1591–1604.

Bovens, M., Geveke, H., & Vries, J. D. (1993). Strikt vertrouwelijk: lekken in het openbaar bestuur. *Beleid en Maatschappij*, 20(2), 61–80.

Brands, H. W. (2004). George Bush and the Gulf War of 1991. *Presidential Studies Quarterly*, 34(1), 113–131.

Brattström, A., & Richtnér, A. (2014). Good cop–bad cop: Trust, control, and the lure of integration. *Journal of Product Innovation Management*, 31(3), 584–598.

Bruijn, H. de. (2017). *The art of framing: How politicians convince us that they are right*. Haarlem, the Netherlands: Etopia BV.

Bruijn, H. de, Heuvelhof, E. F. ten, & Kuit, M. (1999). *Sport 7: de opkomst en ondergang van een Nederlandse sportzender*. Antwerp, Belgium: Aristos Uitgeverij.

Bruijn, H. de, Heuvelhof, E. F. ten, & Veld, R. J. in 't (2000). *Procesmanagement. Over procesontwerp en besluitvorming*. the Netherlands: Academic Service.

Bruijn, H. de, Heuvelhof, E. F. ten, & Veld, R. J. in't. (2010). *Process management: Why project management fails in complex decision making processes*. (2nd ed.). Berlin: Springer-Verlag.

Buchanan, D. A., & Boddy, D. (1992). *The expertise of the change agent: Public performance and backstage activity*. Upper Saddle River, NJ: Prentice Hall.

Burandt, S., Gralla, F., & John, B. (2015). Actor analysis in case studies for (regional) sustainable development. *Envigogika*, 10(1), 1–14. doi:10.14712/18023061.433

Busch, P.-O., & Jörgens, H. (2001). Breaking the deadlock: voluntary agreements and regulatory measures in German waste management policy, Paper presented at

European Consortium for Political Research Joint Sessions Institute of Political Studies, Grenoble, France.

Bush, G. H. W., & Scowcroft, B. (1998). *A world transformed.* New York: Knopf.

Business Week (1999).

Cameron, K. S. (1986). Effectiveness as paradox: Consensus and conflict in conceptions of organizational effectiveness. *Management Science,* 32(5), 539–553.

Castells, M. (2011). *The rise of the network society: The information age: Economy, society, and culture* (Vol. 1). Hoboken, NJ: John Wiley & Sons.

Coleman, J. S. (1971). Control of collectivities and the power of a collectivity to act. In B. Lieberman (Ed.) *Social choice* (pp. 269–300). Amsterdam: Gordon and Breach.

Commission of the European Communities. (2000). *Implementing the Community strategy to reduce CO2 emissions from cars: First annual report on the effectiveness of the strategy (COM/2000/0615).* Brussels: European Parliament Publications Office.

Cross, J. G. (1977). Negotiation as a learning process. *Journal of Conflict Resolution,* 21(4), 581–606.

Dixit, A. K., & Nalebuff, B. J. (1991). *Thinking strategically: The competitive edge in business, politics, and everyday life.* New York and London: W.W. Norton & Company.

Donaldson, L. (1990). The ethereal hand: Organizational economics and management theory. *Academy of Management Review,* 15(3), 369–381.

Duh, M., Belak, J., & Milfelner, B. (2010). Core values, culture and ethical climate as constitutional elements of ethical behaviour: Exploring differences between family and non-family enterprises. *Journal of Business Ethics,* 97(3), 473–489.

Engels, F. (1890). Brief an Joseph Bloch. *Iring Fetscher, Hg., Karl Marx-Friedrich Engels, Studienausgabe in,* 4, 226–228.

Enserink, B., Kwakkel, J., Bots, P., Hermans, L., Thissen, W., & Koppenjan, J. (2010). *Policy analysis of multi-actor systems.* The Hague, the Netherlands: Eleven International Publishing.

Fatima, S. S., Wooldridge, M., & Jennings, N. R. (2006). Multi–issue negotiation with deadlines. *Journal of Artificial Intelligence Research,* 27, 381–417.

Fili, A. (2014). Business angel–venture negotiation in the post-investment relationship: the use of the good cop, bad cop strategy. *Venture Capital,* 16(4), 309–325.

Flamini, F. (2007). First things first? The agenda formation problem for multi–issue committees. *Journal of Economic Behavior & Organization,* 63(1), 138–157.

Flinders, M., & Buller, J. (2006). Depoliticisation: Principles, tactics and tools. *British Politics,* 1(3), 293–318.

Flyvbjerg, B. (2007). Truth and lies about megaprojects [speech]. Retrieved from http://flyvbjerg.plan.aau.dk/Publications2007/InauguralTUD21PRINT72dpi.pdf

Frey, B. S., Benz, M., & Stutzer, A. (2004). Introducing procedural utility: Not only what, but also how matters. *Journal of Institutional and Theoretical Economics,* 160(3), 377–401.

Granovetter, M. S. (1973). The strength of weak ties. *American Journal of Sociology,* 78(6), 1360–1380.

Guba, E. G., & Lincoln, Y. S. (1989). *Fourth generation evaluation.* Thousand Oaks, CA: Sage Publications.

Guinée, J. B. (2002). Handbook on life cycle assessment operational guide to the ISO standards. *The International Journal of Life Cycle Assessment,* 7(5), 311–313.

Hekster, O. (2005). *Beelden van macht.* Nijmegen, the Netherlands: Thieme MediaCenter.

Heuvelhof, E. F. ten (2016). *Strategisch gedrag in netwerken. Wat het is, hoe we het ontwikkelen, wat we ervan moeten vinden.* The Hague, the Netherlands: Boombestuurskunde.

Hollander-Blumoff, R., & Tyler, T. R. (2008). Procedural justice in negotiation: Procedural fairness, outcome acceptance, and integrative potential. *Law & Social Inquiry,* 33(2), 473–500.

Huntington, S. P. (1981). *American Politics: The Promise of Disharmony.* Cambridge, MA: Belknap Press.

Jasanoff, S. (2009). *The fifth branch: Science advisers as policymakers.* Cambridge, MA: Harvard University Press.

Jay, M. (2010). *The virtues of mendacity: On lying in politics.* Charlottesville: University of Virginia Press.

Keltner, D. (2016). *The power paradox: How we gain and lose influence.* New York: Penguin Press.

Kickert, W. J., Klijn, E.-H., & Koppenjan, J. F. (1997). *Managing complex networks: Strategies for the public sector.* Thousand Oaks, CA: Sage Publications.

Kim, P. H., & Fragale, A. R. (2005). Choosing the path to bargaining power: An empirical comparison of BATNAs and contributions in negotiation. *Journal of Applied Psychology,* 90(2), 373–381.

Kingdon, J. W. (1984). *Longman Classics in Political Science: Vol. 45. Agendas, alternatives, and public policies.* Boston, MA: Little, Brown.

Kissinger, H. (1994). *Diplomacy.* New York: Simon & Schuster.

Klijn, E.-H., Edelenbos, J., Kort, M., & van Twist, M. (2008). Facing management choices: an analysis of managerial choices in 18 complex environmental public-private partnership projects. *International Review of Administrative Sciences,* 74(2), 251–282.

Krummenacher, H. (1985). *Internationale normen und krisen: Die normative dimension internationaler politik* (Unpublished doctoral dissertation). University of Zürich.

Lees, C. (2005). Environmental policy: the law of diminishing returns? In S. Green & W.E. Patterson (Eds.) *Governance in contemporary Germany: The semisovereign state revisited* (pp. 212–238). Cambridge: Cambridge University Press.

Li, J.-R., Li, H.-Y., & Jiang, Z.-C. (2008). The analyze of the launch window for space rescue mission. *Journal of National University of Defense Technology,* (1), 10–14.

Lidskog, R., & Sundqvist, G. (2004). From consensus to credibility: New challenges for policy-relevant science. *Innovation: The European Journal of Social Science Research,* 17(3), 205–226.

Lindblom, C. E. (1959). The science of "muddling through". *Public Administration Review,* 79–88.

Liu, M. (2009). The intrapersonal and interpersonal effects of anger on negotiation strategies: A cross-cultural investigation. *Human Communication Research,* 35(1), 148–169.

Lorenz, E. H. (1991). Neither friends nor strangers: Informal networks of subcontracting in French industry. In G. Thompson, J. Francis, R. Levacic, & J. Mitchell (Eds) *Markets, hierarchies and networks: The coordination of social life* (pp. 183–192). Thousand Oaks, CA: Sage Publications.

Lubben, S. J. (2015). The board's duty to keep its options open. *University of Illinois Law Review,* (2), 817–829.

Mauss, M. (1990). *The gift: The form and reason for exchange in archaic societies.* (W.D. Halls, Trans.). Abingdon: Routledge. (Original work published 1950)

Milgrom, P. R. (1984). Axelrod's "The Evolution of Cooperation" [Review of the book The Evolution of Cooperation by R. Axelrod]. *RAND Journal of Economics*, 15(2), 305–309.

Moen, R., & Norman, C. (2006). Evolution of the PDCA cycle. Retrieved from www. westga.edu/~dturner/PDCA.pdf

Monnikhof, R. A. H. (2006). *Policy analysis for participatory policy making* (Unpublished doctoral thesis). Delft University of Technology, the Netherlands.

Morgan, G. (1986). *Images of organization*. Beverly Hills, CA: Sage Publications.

Morgan, M. G. (2016). Opinion: Climate policy needs more than muddling. *Proceedings of the National Academy of Sciences*, 113(9), 2322–2324.

Muthusamy, S. K., & White, M. A. (2005). Learning and knowledge transfer in strategic alliances: a social exchange view. *Organization Studies*, 26(3), 415–441.

Ordóñez, L. D., Schweitzer, M. E., Galinsky, A. D., & Bazerman, M. H. (2009). Goals gone wild: The systematic side effects of overprescribing goal setting. *The Academy of Management Perspectives*, 23(1), 6–16.

Peters, B. G. (1998). Managing horizontal government: The politics of co-ordination. *Public Administration*, 76(2), 295–311.

Petts, J. (2003). Barriers to deliberative participation in EIA: Learning from waste policies, plans and projects. *Journal of Environmental Assessment Policy and Management*, 5(03), 269–293.

Public Administration Select Committee Eighth Report. (2002). *'These unfortunate events': Lessons of recent events at the former DTLR*. London: Parliament House of Commons.

Quinn, R. E., & Rohrbaugh, J. (1983). A spatial model of effectiveness criteria: Towards a competing values approach to organizational analysis. *Management Science*, 29(3), 363–377.

Ravetz, I. (1999). Editorial: What is post-normal science. *Futures: The Journal of Policy, Planning and Future Studies*, 31(7), 647–653.

Rawls, J. (1971). *A theory of justice*. Cambridge, MA: Harvard University Press.

Rhodes, R. A. W. (1991). Interorganizational networks and control. In F.-X. Kaufmann (Ed.), *The public sector: Challenges for coordination and learning* (pp. 525–533). Berlin: Walter de Gruyter.

Rittel, H. W., & Webber, M. M. (1973). Dilemmas in a general theory of planning. *Policy Sciences*, 4(2), 155–169.

Rosenthal, U. (1980). De machtsparadox: latente machtsuitoefening en geanticipeerde reacties. *Beleid en Maatschappij*, 7, 292–296.

Scharpf, F. W. (1978). Interorganizational policy studies: issues, concepts and perspectives. In K. Hanf & F. W. Scharpf (Eds), *Inter-organizational policymaking: Limits to coordination and central control* (pp. 345–370). Thousand Oaks, CA: Sage Publications.

Scharpf, F. W. (1997). *Games real actors play: Actor-centered institutionalism in policy research*. Boulder, CO: Westview Press.

Schelling, T. C. (1960). *The strategy of conflict*. Cambridge, MA: Harvard University Press.

Schelling, T. C. (1978). Altruism, meanness, and other potentially strategic behaviors. *American Economic Review*, 68(2), 229–230.

Schön, D. (1983). *The reflective practitioner: How professionals think in action*. New York: Basic Books.

Shephard, R. W., & Färe, R. (1974). The law of diminishing returns. *Zeitschrift für Nationalökonomie*, 34(1–2), 69–90.

Simon, G. L., Bumpus, A. G., & Mann, P. (2012). Win-win scenarios at the climate–development interface: Challenges and opportunities for stove replacement programs through carbon finance. *Global Environmental Change*, 22(1), 275–287.

Simon, H. A. (1957). *Administrative behavior: A study of decision-making processes in administrative organization* (2nd ed.). New York: Macmillan,

Sinaceur, M., Van Kleef, G. A., Neale, M. A., Adam, H., & Haag, C. (2011). Hot or cold: Is communicating anger or threats more effective in negotiation? *Journal of Applied Psychology*, 96(5), 1018–1032.

Teisman, G. R. (2000). Models for research into decision-making processes: On phases, streams and decision-making rounds. *Public Administration*, 78(4), 937–956.

Thatcher, M. (2004). Winners and losers in Europeanisation: Reforming the national regulation of telecommunications. *West European Politics*, 27(2), 284–309.

Todo, Y., Matous, P., & Inoue, H. (2016). The strength of long ties and the weakness of strong ties: Knowledge diffusion through supply chain networks. *Research Policy*, 45(9), 1890–1906.

Vuori, V. (2006). Methods of defining business information needs. In M. Maula, M. Hannula, M. Seppä, & J. Tommila (Eds), *Frontiers of e-Business Research ICEB+ eBRF Conference Proceedings, 28.11.–2.12.2006, Tampere, Finland* (pp. 311–319). Tampere, Finland: University of Technology & University of Tampere.

Waterman, R. W., & Meier, K. J. (1998). Principal-agent models: an expansion? *Journal of Public Administration Research and Theory*, 8(2), 173–202.

Weening, H. M. (2006). *Smart cities: Omgaan met onzekerheid*. Delft, the Netherlands: Uitgeverij Eburon.

Weible, C., Sabatier, P. A., & Lubell, M. (2004). A comparison of a collaborative and top-down approach to the use of science in policy: Establishing marine protected areas in California. *Policy Studies Journal*, 32(2), 187–209.

Williamson, O. E. (1985). *The economic institutions of capitalism: Firms, markets, relational contracting*. New York: Free Press.

Williamson, O. E. (1989). Handbooks in Economics: Vol. 10. Transaction cost economics. In R. Schmalensee, R. Willig (Eds), *Handbook of industrial organization*, (Vol. 1) (pp. 135–182). Amsterdam, the Netherlands: North-Holland Publishing.

Woolley, J. T., & McGinnis, M. V. (1999). The politics of watershed policymaking. *Policy Studies Journal*, 27(3), 578–594.

Zenou, Y. (2015). A dynamic model of weak and strong ties in the labor market. *Journal of Labor Economics*, 33(4), 891–932.

Index

Note: Page numbers in **boldface** indicate tables and those in *italics* indicate figures.